# YOU CAN'T BE SERIOUS:

## An inner-city teacher a-muses about school and life

*To Lauren —*

*Enjoy the book !*

*Best wishes —*

*Larry Berbiar*

*11/19*

# YOU CAN'T BE SERIOUS:

## An inner-city teacher a-muses about school and life

## Larry Berliner

Published by SRB Books

ISBN: 978-0-9839401-6-6

Cover design by Book Graphics
Original cover art by Paula Bodger
Formatting by Rik: Wild Seas Formatting
(http://WildSeasFormatting.com)

Published October, 2017

Printed in the United States of America

# DEDICATION

This book is dedicated to my amazing wife, Susan, who never lost faith in my ability (and need) to produce something worthwhile. Without her constant nagging, er, encouragement, this book wouldn't have been written. So if for any reason you are dissatisfied, you know who to blame. As for me, Susan is directly or indirectly responsible for everything good in my life.

# ACKNOWLEDGEMENTS

First, I want to thank my wife, Susan, for helping me arrange a series of disjointed ideas into a (hopefully) finished product. She has endured reading this book as editor and proofreader more times than I thought possible, especially with me fighting to hold on to every word.

Thank you, Rich Mintzer, for the time I spent in your Continuing Education comedy course at Westchester Community College. After hearing me read a chapter and talk about my plans for the book, Mr. Mintzer made two suggestions that sharpened and redirected my focus. (See "Introduction.")

Thank you too, dear family and friends, who never stopped asking me about the book and kept reminding me I was writing one. A friend compared its eventual birth to the end of a 10-year pregnancy.

I'm also grateful to two friends and former colleagues who helped me remember some zany events from long ago. (Oh, if I'd only had the good sense to keep a diary!) My good friend, Gene Ehrens, and I were able to put our aging heads together and recall some pretty funny stuff.

Similarly, Paul Cohen, now hundreds of miles away, reminded me of some of our antics by e-mail (when he wasn't bashing President Obama). Paul was also the culprit who devised the Bathroom Standards in Chapter Two.

Finally, I'd like to acknowledge my children, Meredith and David, neither of whom contributed anything to this book.

# TABLE OF CONTENTS

ASIDE TO THE READER......................................................7

INTRODUCTION ..................................................9

IT WAS AN EDUCATION

The Officer's Candidate ....................................... 17

School Daze ......................................................... 35

THE NOT-SO-FINE ART OF COMMUNICATION

Can We Talk?........................................................ 85

Telephone Tag...................................................... 103

Cell Privileges..................................................... 115

LA VIDA LOCA

At Your Service – Not! ....................................... 133

We, The Jury ........................................................ 143

Family Vacations: A Tale Of Two Brothers ..................... 153

TO MY HEALTH

A Shot In The Ass ............................................... 167

No Place Like Om................................................ 175

With A Side Of Effects – To Go............................ 183

AFTERWARD ....................................................... 193

APPENDIX ........................................................... 195

# ASIDE TO THE READER

This book is not that good. I'm not saying my book sucks. It's entertaining, amusing, and sporadically thought-provoking. You might even call it a fun-filled page-turner. But it's not that good. If writing a book is going to consume more than ten years of your life, it should be mentioned with *War and Peace, Gone With the Wind*, or anything by Shakespeare.

So why did it take me so long to tell my stories? Let's just say life got in the way – along with the author's procrastination and a stubborn insistence on rewriting until satisfied. I hope you enjoy the book. Just don't expect Tolstoy, Mitchell, or Shakespeare. It's not that good.

# INTRODUCTION

For more than thirty years, I taught English/Reading to sixth, seventh, and eighth graders in The Bronx, New York. During that time, I also wrote educational material and standardized test questions for grades K – 12 as a freelancer. All the while, I dreamed of one day writing the Great American Novel.

Over the years, ideas crept into my head and I looked forward to featuring them in my book. Some ideas came to me in dreams, some on the treadmill. I wrote some down and misplaced them; others I committed to memory and promptly forgot.

When I finally retired, it was time to release the masterpiece stored piecemeal in my brain and enter the novelist phase of my life. A professional writer with so many great, if disparate, ideas – how could I possibly go wrong?

And so I sat down to write. I developed a couple of chapters, looked them over, and wondered, *Where do I go from here?* I decided to ask Susan, my wife and long-time writing partner, for her impression of what I'd done and where I seemed to be going.

"Give me your honest opinion," I foolishly insisted, though I would gladly have settled for a kind dose of false flattery.

Susan read my work and unfortunately opted for the honest opinion. She tactfully suggested that the reader needed to care about the main character – and she didn't. Upon rereading, I realized I too didn't much care about my main character, his point of view, or where the story seemed to be going.

She added that she also didn't like the dialogue. "It's not realistic." (I didn't recall asking for a second opinion.)

Succeeding attempts at writing my novel confirmed only that I wasn't going to write one. Visions of writing the Great American Novel faded. Dammit, I knew I could write – I'd proven it over the years. But novels were apparently a different animal – one I feared I could never master. I reluctantly resigned myself to creating just educational materials. But it wasn't enough.

Susan suggested I try writing about experiences in and out of school. "You don't have to be a novelist." (Thank God.) "You have a great sense of humor. What about all the funny stories you tell? Why not write them down?"

I knew this was a good idea, but going from the Great American Novel to some goofy stories...My heart just wasn't in it. I also wondered how my sense of humor would translate to the written page.

Meanwhile, after leaving her full-time job, Susan was cleaning out her desk at home and came across a news article about a dust devil that had wreaked havoc in Maine several years earlier. Considering the location, she had assumed Stephen King would jump all over it and write a novel about killer dust. But he hadn't.

Since one of her favorite authors had passed on the opportunity, she decided to give it a try. After writing the first two chapters, she asked me to read her work and give my honest opinion. Although this was not long after telling me my novel sucked, I was determined to be kind.

I read her chapters and thought, *Where did this come from?* As an English major in college, a teacher for over three decades, and someone who could recognize a good story, I knew there would indeed be a novelist in this family, and it wasn't me.

"You've got to write this book," I insisted.

For once, she listened to me and this embryonic literary exercise evolved into her first published novel, imaginatively titled *Dust*. No ordinary dust devil, this malevolent whirlwind terrorizes a condo community.

*Dust* was followed by *Peachwood Lake*, where a demonic fish makes Jaws look like a goitered guppy; *The Disappearance*, for those who enjoy time travel with a touch of *The Sting; Corsonia*, a small Nevada town whose inhabitants have unknowingly forfeited their minds; and a book of paranormal short stories, *The Sea Crystal and Other Weird Tales*.

For each of these riveting books, I was the editor-in-chief and designated proofreader. I drove her to book-signing events, took pictures, handed out bookmarks, and made change for her customers. I had become a novelist by marriage. I was proud of my role as supporter of the arts – but something was missing.

All the while, Susan knew there was a book in me crying to be born. Throughout her non-hostile takeover as the family novelist, she kept reminding me to return to my writing.

Reluctantly, I went back and edited an earlier attempt at a humorous tale and then wrote another chapter. We agreed they were good, but that I could make them better. I would make them better.

And so I modified my dream. Since the Great American Novel was off the table, I would simply aim to write something I could be proud of – not necessarily something to entertain an audience (though I wouldn't object to it becoming a best-seller). I would write a book about my experiences and observations, and I would write it for me. I would write something I was satisfied with, something to leave behind, something that said,

"Larry was here."

It would be like carving your name in a school desk or in an old oak tree. Remember the prison librarian in *The Shawshank Redemption* who spent most of his life behind bars? Shortly after his release, he carved, "Brooks was here" in the ceiling of his room in a halfway house and then hanged himself. That's what I'm talking about – without the hanging part.

So I wrote a few more chapters and they were pretty good. But even after some serious editing, I doubted they would be my notch in the tree. I felt like a chronicler with the skill to recognize and record the humor in everyday situations. But something was still missing.

Then one day Susan (Who else?) suggested my son and I take a comedy-writing course at Westchester Community College – mainly to encourage David, who had developed some funny stand-up routines. And perhaps I could stumble upon a way to improve my stories.

The instructor, Rich Mintzer, had extensive professional writing experience, having authored or ghosted more than eighty published titles and having written for radio and TV shows, including Rosie O'Donnell.

On the last day of class, we were all given a chance to perform our stand-up routines. Instead of standing up, I chose to remain seated and read a chapter from the book that was going nowhere.

Mr. Mintzer complimented me on my work and made two suggestions. After learning my book would be titled, *Are You Serious?* he told me I needed more. "This title says nothing." Together we decided on *Are You Serious? Memories, observations, and reflections of an inner-city teacher, both in and out of school.* (I later changed the title to *You Can't Be Serious* because of the double entendre and shortened the tag line.) At least now people would know what the book they didn't want to buy was about.

His second, and most helpful, observation was that my story was too literal. He explained that while the best comedy comes from real life experiences, I could take some liberties. No one knows – or cares – if these stories are verbatim. This was not an autobiography or even a series of typical memoirs. If adding or tweaking material enhanced the narrative and/or the humor – go for it. Leave out details that don't contribute to the story. (I actually taught in two inner-city schools – but who cares?)

With this in mind, in addition to being a humorous chronicler, I became a more creative writer – although some of the wackiest incidents are virtually accurate and, for the most part, the exaggeration is transparent.

But now I was writing, remembering, and creating at the same time. I had the option of embellishing for amusement where it improved the narrative. Also, except where noted, the names have been changed to protect – me.

I still had to rekindle my enthusiasm after too many layoffs. But after countless rewrites and interruptions, I finally experienced my "Fonzie moment." Remember the old sit-com *Happy Days* when The Fonz looks in the mirror, comb in hand, and instead of combing, just spreads his hands and says, "Ayyy!"?

While I could have rewritten this book for the rest of my life, I finally felt I could look at it, back away from the computer, and say, "Ayyy!"

So here it is. I'm satisfied. But I wish it didn't have to take so damned long to write. It's not THAT good.

# IT WAS AN EDUCATION

# THE OFFICER'S CANDIDATE

"They also serve..."
– John Milton

**I went off to college** in the early 1960s, if you can call forty minutes on the D subway train "going off" to college. But there was a sense of pride in attending City College of New York (CCNY) before open admission, when an incoming freshman was still required to have a working brain.

## Uncle Sam Wants Who?

Like most of my contemporaries, when I was 18, my working brain wasn't my favorite organ. So when I saw pictures of smiling young men in uniform with gorgeous girls draped over their arms, I decided to look into the college's Reserve Officers' Training Corps (ROTC) program.

In the '60s, young scholars joined the ROTC to satisfy one of two burning needs: to command a platoon of unsuccessful draft dodgers or to meet girls. I couldn't read a map, was deathly afraid of guns, and never fantasized about being a leader of men. But I fantasized about girls constantly. And people said I'd look good in a uniform.

# Sign Me Up!

At registration, along with Comp Lit 101, math, science, etc., I signed up for ROTC – a one-credit elective course. Frankly, I never thought about the military ramifications of my decision. But I did look pretty good in the uniform and I knew the ROTC could definitely help me meet girls.

For three years I attended ROTC class, participated in drills, saluted officers, and strutted around campus in full military regalia (except for when I tweaked protocol by taking off my jacket and rolling up my sleeves to play ball with friends). And I always escorted an attractive date to the military balls.

I generally did nothing to either distinguish or embarrass myself during the weekly ROTC routines. I could handle the field drills (though I was usually about a half-beat off) and the classes were mostly mundane. I learned to dismantle and reassemble an M-1 rifle, except for two or three leftover pieces, which I would hide in my uniform jacket.

After class, I discovered I wasn't the only cadet with the mechanical expertise of a chimpanzee on meds. Suspicious jingling noises at dismissal suggested this next wave of potential commissioned officers had amassed enough "spare" rifle parts to launch its own mission of mass destruction.

# Welcome to "The Gap"

Those of us who, after three years, remained faithful to our dreams of battlefield heroism – or who had not yet met the girls of our dreams – were invited to Summer Camp, which convened in the quaint little town of Indiantown Gap, Pennsylvania. There I spent six weeks of my life, proving beyond doubt that our country's military defense would be better served if left in the hands of others.

At the "Gap" I had an opportunity to meet and mingle with young men from different parts of the country, many of whom, to my surprise, had never met a Jew. One sheltered soul actually apologized for expecting to see horns when I removed my cap. Others, I'm sure, wrote home about their proximity to a real live Jew-boy. (My upbringing in the East Bronx had created the illusion that we were an ethnic majority. Even my three years at CCNY suggested Jews were, at the very least, a significant minority. Who knew?)

But my summer camp debacle was not an indictment of these narrow-minded, ignorant bastards. This story in no way chronicles one man's heroic struggle to overcome the pitfalls of prejudice. I wouldn't have distinguished myself that summer if the entire experience had been sponsored by B'nai B'rith.

## No Time For – This Sergeant

My platoon leader was Sergeant Nagle, a career soldier who must have once fancied himself some sort of modern gladiator. But the ravages of war and time had clearly taken their toll. Sergeant Nagle tried, unsuccessfully, to conceal the fact that over the years he had apparently absorbed too many hits in the line of duty. He was a driven, impersonal, joyless man with the charisma of a rotting log, who substituted spitting on the ground for commas when he addressed his troops.

He also displayed a noticeable twitch, which intensified with his mood, making me question his ability to lead young draft dodgers into serious combat. Since the twitch became more evident as he glared at a cadet's fumbling efforts to sort out the component parts of an M-1 rifle, I wondered how he had fared in the heat of battle, where, to the best of my knowledge, both sides were required to employ fully assembled weapons.

I could easily envision Sergeant Nagle as a twitchy Don

Knotts on drugs. Yet it was his job to transform this band of inexperienced but enthusiastic undergraduates into a cohesive unit of well-trained, highly competent – or at least credible – commissioned officers.

And Sergeant Nagle did not take his assignment lightly. He turned ballistic when any of us called a rifle a "gun." After a two-spit, multi-twitch tirade, Sergeant Nagle made the offender hold his crotch (his own – not the Sergeant's) in one hand, his rifle in the other, and repeat: "This is my rifle; this is my gun. This is for fighting; this is for fun." The goofy rhyme was actually kind of funny, but Sergeant Nagle didn't do funny. He saw it as a kind of confessional.

"Louder! Again!" (spit, twitch)

While I realized a rifle was a soldier's right arm, Sergeant Nagle seemed to have an unnatural affinity for his M-1. Rumor had it he even slept with his rifle. Rumor also suggested some of his battle wounds were inflicted by a middle-of–the-night rendezvous with his metaphorical "arm."

## The Drill of It All

Rifle drills were a large part of our daily routine. Fortunately, they did not involve any of the sergeant's uniquely creative positions. For our crew, standard moves were enough of a challenge. We were so dysfunctional, I was actually competitive in these drills.

In those early days of summer camp, I might have blended in seamlessly with my fellow trainees, except I couldn't seem to avoid drawing the sergeant's unsolicited attention. One hot afternoon, I loosened my tie and collar and triggered a highly spirited, spittle-laden shout down. Requesting fluids only exacerbated the situation.

"Drinking water is for sissies!" (spit, twitch)

A handkerchief to mop my brow?

"Real men don't towel off!"

And so it went.

## Now Cut That Out!

Once we were deemed sufficiently proficient with our M-1 rifles, Sergeant Nagle decided we were ready to move on to the next phase of our crash course in matters military. I didn't see how we were ready to "move on" to anything. If our rifles had been properly loaded, the field would have been strewn with bodies like the battle scene from *Gone With the Wind*.

But on we moved. The next item on my federally-imposed bucket list was Bayonet Drill. I'm sure this activity could have been an entertaining addition to our routine, but for some reason the organizers of this instructional summer camp decided to attach real bayonets to our M-1 rifles. Rubber knives could easily have been purchased at any department store or discount warehouse and I'm sure the army would have gotten a good price for buying in bulk. However, these uniformed party-poopers opted for the real thing – authentic, long, very sharp knives, designed to cut deeply and inflict serious injury.

I kept these heretic thoughts to myself as we novices dutifully formed two lines facing each other with our genuine weapons bared, ready to engage in mock combat. I sensed a wide discrepancy in the range of enthusiasm from, "I'm ready to cut your mother f____n' head off!" to, "Someone could get hurt here!"

Sure enough, my "mock" opponent zigged just when the situation clearly called for an abrupt zag and my authentic bayonet opened an authentically ghastly wound on his right arm. "Sergeant!" I called. "This man is hurt!"

Sergeant Nagle ambled over with the urgent concern of a grazing cow and blurted my daily reprimand. "Why are you wasting my time, soldier? This man is your enemy."

"No, he's not. He's my friend..."

"Your answer is, 'No excuse, Sergeant.' That is your only response."

"No excuse, Sergeant," I dutifully replied.

But there was more. "You don't have any friends on that side of the line, Mister," Sergeant Nagle continued. "What are you going to do if you cut Charlie?" (spit) "Ask if he's OK? Get a band-aid?"

Immediately forgetting my latest lesson in military etiquette, I blurted: "This isn't Charlie, Sergeant. It's John Gibbons. I..."

"Are you ridiculing me, soldier, or are you just plain stupid?"

I waited patiently for a third choice. When I realized there was none forthcoming, I stood quietly in place, hoping the question was rhetorical. (The sergeant's "no excuse" option didn't seem to apply.)

"I'm waiting, Mister!"

Obviously Sergeant Nagle didn't do rhetorical. He wanted me to answer the damn question. I suspected it would go better for me if I opted for choice number two. "I'm stupid, sir."

"That's 'Sergeant'!" (mega twitch)

"I'm stupid, Sergeant." I guess that sounded a little better, but the uneasy silence that followed seemed to suggest it was still my turn. "I'm stupid, Sergeant," I obediently repeated. "But sir, John is really bleeding..."

"Step back, Berliner. Mr. Gibbons, are you able to continue?"

"Yes, Sergeant."

*Sure he is. If he doesn't bleed out.*

"Sampson, get your ass over here and replace Berliner. Gibbons, put a rag on your arm. You're bleeding on government issue. Berliner, double time to the barracks. I'll deal with you later."

"Yes, sir...Sergeant!" As I ran, I thought about poor John Gibbons who couldn't defend himself against a Jewish pacifist from The Bronx, facing off against "Crazy Neville Sampson" (the man voted most likely to level a village for no apparent reason), with one arm virtually useless and the other holding a bloody cloth.

## My Time to Shine

After about two weeks, the reigning powers determined we were ready to assume command responsibility. Each day, a highly unqualified trainee (or two) took a turn as squad leader. On the morning of my anointment, I lined my men in single file, facing me, just outside the barracks. They stood dutifully at attention, obviously anticipating words of inspiration or at least some meaningful direction.

Instead I ordered them to hand over any excess toilet paper to their leader du jour. (I knew that in the field we were supposed to utilize what nature provided, but two days earlier, nature had provided another officer's candidate with a serious and somewhat embarrassing case of poison ivy, so I decided to use what Charmin provided.) After pooling enough toilet paper to blow my nose, I dismissed my frugal followers.

Later that morning, I was handed a map and told my squad's mission was to take Hill Whatchamacallit. Without allowing me time to turn the map right side up, Sergeant Nagle demanded I immediately familiarize myself with the terrain. I stared at what appeared to be some convoluted third world country board game. Then the Sergeant bellowed, "Blah! Blah! Blah!" (spit) "Is that understood?"

Without missing a beat or understanding a word, I responded, "Yes, Sergeant!" although my map reading skills were rivaled only by my sense of direction. (Back in the real world in the days before GPS, when I found myself driving in circles, I was glad to be able to navigate from one "helpful" gas station attendant to another.) As I dutifully perused the map, thinking this military hodgepodge would intrigue Magellan, I hoped to find an "X" on a hill or at least a big red dot labeled, "You are here."

Although I had lost much of my credibility with the earlier toilet paper roundup, my squad listened attentively as I explained how they would spread out, slither along the ground, and at my signal, charge the hill, and (hopefully) carry out our mission.

An hour later, these obedient officers-in-training spread, slithered, charged and – to everyone's surprise – with remarkably little resistance, captured the damn hill. Somehow, we had achieved our objective.

I proudly faced my giddy squad and spoke words I had always dreamed of saying – along with, "Let's make this a true Daily Double": "Take five. Smoke if you got 'em!" I then assumed the well-earned position of a conquering hero and stretched out on the grass, overlooking my newly-acquired terrain.

My reverie was broken by the blinding reflection of sunlight off a pair of outrageously over-polished shoes. "Squad Leader Berliner!" raged a full-bird colonel.

I jumped to attention and saluted. "Yes, sir!"

"What was your mission?"

"Take the hill, sir!"

"What hill, Mister?"

"This hill?" I prayed.

"Do you see that hill beyond the Ramafras trees?"

*No, but...*"Yes, sir."

"Do all these hills look alike to you, Mister?"

*Carbon copies.* "No, sir!"

"You took the wrong damn hill, Mister! How the hell could you take the wrong damn hill?"

"No excuse, sir."

I resisted the temptation to state the obvious: "*It was easy, sir. No one was shooting back at us.*"

## Oh, Shoot!

Sergeant Nagle's voice was among the last things I wanted to hear at 3 a.m. along with, "Your house is on fire!," "Stick 'em up!," and, "This is a genital inspection!" But there he was, standing in the middle of our suddenly well-lit room.

"You misfits are wasting the night sleeping!" he bellowed. (spit)

*Who was going to clean that up?*

"We gotta be at the rifle range in twenty minutes!" the sergeant continued. "What better way to spend this beautiful night?"

I quietly suggested several, but my unreasonably zealous comrades were practically dressed and ready to go by the time I found the first of two matching shoes. I tried to rub the sticky stuff from the corner of my eye, then realized it hadn't yet had time to form. Generally a lousy sleeper, I was just getting used to this bunkmate setting. Naturally, the first night I was experiencing something resembling real sleep would be designated for target practice.

I couldn't help thinking that, at this time on a good date night in the world I'd left behind, I would be slipping into bed and reviewing the highlights of my evening. Now I was stumbling out of my bunk, groping for my gear ("Oops, sorry Pete"), and preparing to trek to a damn rifle range.

"Berliner! Are you ready to move out?" (spit, twitch)

"Yes, Sergeant!" I lied.

Sergeant Nagle strutted out of the room, deftly avoiding

27

the wet reminder of his untimely intrusion.

"Why three o'clock in the morning?" I wondered out loud. "The damn range will still be there at sun-up."

"We gonna do most of our fighting at night," someone volunteered.

"I know. But this is our first time. Wouldn't it help to be able to see?"

"By the time we arrive and deploy, the sun will be rising," another voice chimed in.

"Couldn't we maybe let the sun rise and then go there and deploy?"

"Get with it, Berlinger."

"That's Berliner."

"We're gonna f____n' shoot our guns!"

*Guns? Didn't you mean rifles? Oh, Sergeant!*

"We're gettin' live ammo!"

*Live ammo?*

"Some day we'll be shooting the shit out of real live Commies!"

(Historical note: In the 1960s, the communist Soviet Union posed our greatest military threat.)

"They won't be live when we get through with them!"

(Group laugh, a couple of hoots, an artificial burp, two genuine farts...)

"We'll be taking f____n' target practice on those Commies, Nips, and..."

(Historical note #2: "Nips?" We had been at peace with the Japanese for twenty years.)

Clearly there was a palpable surge of "patriotism" growing within the ranks, though one could detect a hint of braggadocio creeping into the battle cries:

"Some day Ahm gonna be a he-ro."

*Some day I'll find my shoes.*

Somehow, I managed to fall in without falling on my face and headed out with the muddled masses yearning to be "heroes."

## Home on the Range

After our drenching stroll (Did I mention it was raining?) we arrived at the rifle range. Another platoon was standing at attention, listening attentively to an expletive-laced detailed explanation of how they had disgraced their uniforms, their families, and everything else from God and country to Philly cheesesteaks.

Meanwhile, two army corporals demonstrated how to aim at and perhaps hit a target I could barely see. Then another corporal scooped up and replaced the battered targets, marched to the end of the row and stood there like Vanna White, obediently waiting for someone to buy a vowel.

Just as the sun was breaking through the clouds and I was beginning to master the art of dozing on my feet, I heard that familiar voice: "Spread out, you misfits!" (spit) "Assume the prone position!" I recalled that prone had been my position when I assumed I'd be spending the night in bed.

Then the two corporals dutifully handed each of us three rounds of live ammunition. *Holy shit! I hope I didn't leave out a piece of my M-1. This damn thing could blow up in my face!*

"Load your weapons!"

*It doesn't fit.*

"Ready!"

*Not really.*

"Aim!"

*Aha! Now where's the damn target?*

"Fire!"

*Oh, shit!* I closed my eyes, pulled the trigger, and prayed. As the bullet flew from my rifle-gun, I could only hope I'd hit something. If I did, it surely wasn't the target, which was still in pristine condition. Happy to be alive, I let out a sigh of relief.

"Ready!"

*Are you kidding?*

"Aim!"

*I need a bullet.*

"Fire!"

*With what? I guess I missed that round.*

"Ready!"

*OK. Now I'm ready.*

"Aim!"

*I see it.*

"Fire!"

*I fired.*

That ended the three required rounds of target practice.

As I was about to assume another position, I heard the word, "Fire!" *What happened to, "Ready, Aim"?* Since I had a leftover bullet, I fired, much to the surprise of Corporal Vanna who had just begun to remove the targets. My shot apparently posed no threat to the bull's-eye, but sailed remarkably close to the corporal's ear, instantly transforming him from a casual observer to an active participant moving with renewed purpose.

"Who the hell shot after the cease fire?" an officer raged.

*Someone said, "cease"?*

I was immediately thrown under the bus.

*Oh, look.* Those shiny shoes were before me once again.

"Attention!"

I snapped to attention and saluted. "Yes, sir!"

"Do you know what the word 'cease fire' means, Mister?"

I couldn't bring myself to tell him it was two words.

"Yes, sir. 'Don't shoot.'"

"What did you do?"

"I shot."

"Why the hell did you shoot?"

"No excuse, sir."

"'No excuse'! Is that what you want me to tell Corporal Clinger's widow? 'No excuse'?"

*Now wait a minute. Last week, I was scolded for giving a reason. Last week, the "only answer" was "no excuse." Make up your minds. What the hell is the right answer?*

## On the Road Again

To sleep, perchance to...

"Roll call, you misfits!" (spit)

*Uh, oh. This is gonna be close.*

"Ackerman!"

"Here, Sergeant!"

*Why couldn't my name be Zellman?*

"Barkley!"

"Here, Sergeant!"

I slipped unnoticed into the rear of the formation.

"Berliner!"

"Here, Sergeant!"

After affirming we were all present and accounted for, Sergeant Nagle announced, "We're going out to set up a bivouac. You misfits even know what a bivouac is? Heh, heh." (spit)

Somehow the sergeant could laugh out loud without projecting the slightest hint of joy.

"Line up! Double file! Head out!"

And so we headed out. After logging the required miles of marching, jogging, climbing, and crawling, we reached the designated bivouac site and lined up in the rain (of course) for our mid-day meal. We were each served some really foul-smelling potatoes (*How do you destroy potatoes?*), something off-green, and a barely flexible piece of leathery brown stuff that I heard someone call steak.

When I started to eat, I realized that, in my haste to join the formation, I had neglected to pack my dining knife, which was understandable since we had never been served anything that needed to be cut. My fork and spoon were of little use as I contemplated my assault on this dirt-brown culinary mutant. It wasn't something you could cut with a fork – a chainsaw maybe.

But I was hungry, sitting on the wet ground, staring at my rain-drenched food threatening to float away – except for the "steak," which would require a forklift to shift its position on the tray. Tired of watching others enthusiastically cutting their food (except for three faint-of-stomach trainees retching in the nearby bushes – ah, the ambiance), I employed my own barbaric version of a forklift as I stabbed the steak with my fork and guided it to my mouth with my free hand.

Suddenly, I was blinded by a burst of light that could only come from – shoes! *How the hell did he get them to shine in the rain?*

"Is this how you eat at home, Mister?"

I snapped to attention, yet again, and saluted. "No, sir!" *We sit around a table where there's hardly ever any mud.*

"You're a disgrace! Why do you have a knife in your backpack?"

*Actually...*

"How the hell do you expect to be an officer in this man's army?"

*Yeah, right.* By this time, my military aspirations were in freefall and fading fast.

"Yes, sir. No excuse, sir." I remained at attention as I watched the potatoes and greens of my movable feast slide away.

So much for the bivouac.

## He's Reviewing the Situation

When the six-week tour mercifully came to an end, Sergeant Nagle called each of us into his office for a "preliminary review." This would set the stage for the official decision on who among us would make it to the next round – virtually assured of becoming commissioned officers – and who would fall short and return home targeted for the draft immediately upon graduation.

My final verdict had all the suspense of a steel tank match between a shark and a sardine, but my review did take a few unexpected turns:

"At ease, Berliner." (spit)

*Where the hell did that go? He's got a damn spittoon!*

"You know why you're here."

*You wanted me to see if you could hit the bowl?* "Yes, Sergeant."

"Ever hear of Emily Post?"

"Yes, Sergeant."

"Who is she?"

"She writes about manners, Sergeant, but I don't see..."

"From what I hear, your table manners need refining, Mister. You ate a steak in the field with your hands!"

*With all the ammo I've supplied you with in the last six weeks, you fire at me with Emily Post? I took the wrong hill; I nearly killed Corporal Clinger...*"That's it?"

"No, that's not 'it.' You tried to undermine my platoon, Mister!" (spit, twitch)

"Sir...Sergeant, I don't know how anything I did..."

"Your words in the barracks, Mister."

Sporting that humorless grin, he reached into his drawer, took out some papers, and stared at them.

*What's he reading?*

"'On a good night I'm just getting home now. I spit shined my shoes. I hope the S.O.B. is happy. Now I can see my face in the damned shoes. No girls in this rat hole...'" (spit, twitch) "You want more?"

"There's more?"

"There's lots of more." Once again, that humorless smile.

"But, Sergeant, how could you know...?"

"We know everything, hear everything that goes on...."

"You had the place bugged?"

(spit, smile, twitch) "That will be all, Berliner."

"You're an inspiration, Sergeant. A true molder of men." Now I was looking for a place to spit.

## Fork Y'all

After my enlightening review, I returned to the platoon where some of my "barracks buddies" feigned a passing interest in my current status. However, most were engaged in mock combat, arguing vehemently over the tactics they presumed to have perfected and over who had benefited most (and least) from the summer camp experience.

I loved my country just as much as those self-indulgent six-week wonders. But I knew I would have to serve in different ways – ways that didn't include touching live ammunition, demonstrating map-reading skills, cutting people with knives, or attacking steak with a fork.

# SCHOOL DAZE

"The secret of teaching is to appear to have known all your life
what you learned this afternoon."
– Anonymous

**Nestled securely in the armpit** of the South Bronx, the closely-knit community of Hunt's Point has thrived for hundreds of years. However, during the mid-to-late twentieth century, people drove miles out of their way to avoid this historic slice of Americana for fear of having to stop their cars and (God forbid!) open their windows. This notorious setting was "celebrated" in the 1981 movie, *Fort Apache, The Bronx*.

More than a decade earlier, I applied for my first teaching job at a middle school in the heart of this bastion of education and free enterprise. Fresh out of graduate school and flushed with anticipation of gainful employment, I never considered the added pressure of beginning my rookie season in February, where I would be confronting a sea of piranhas – cleverly disguised as students – soundly entrenched in their positions and remarkably adept at smelling fresh blood in the water.

My application was gobbled up by the administration and, after a brief phone conversation, an interview was arranged with remarkable haste. The next day I sat in the principal's office, flanked by Principal Davis and Assistant Principal Richter, the Language Arts Supervisor, both of whom seemed much too happy to make my acquaintance. After an in-depth interrogation that confirmed I was capable of breathing on my own, they eagerly welcomed me to the staff.

"When could you start?"

"Next week?"

"Good."

## Where's Goldberg?

After completing the intricate hiring process, Mr. Richter handed me a class schedule and a stack of ungraded mid-term exams administered by Morris Goldberg, the teacher I was replacing. "What happened to Mr. Goldberg?" I asked.

The answer came in the form of some uncomfortable mumbling and throat clearing and the not-too-enlightening revelation that Mr. Goldberg, "isn't with us anymore."

Mr. Richter told me to look over the exams to get an idea of my classes' abilities and prior learning. Then he gave me a sample textbook for each class and a rather vague curriculum outline, suggesting I adapt the curriculum to meet the students' needs – whatever that meant. He also said I should try to get them to hang up their coats in the morning.

*"Try to"? Red flag!*

"Use Mr. Goldberg's roll book to take attendance."

*Where's Goldberg?*

"Do the best you can."

*Another red flag.*

## A "Classy" Schedule

My schedule for the spring term included teaching English/Reading to classes 7-4, 7-9, 7-13 and 7-22. Class 7-22 would also be my homeroom responsibility – the class I was expected to restrain each morning and unleash each afternoon.

And this was no haphazard numerical classification. Class 7-22 was, indeed, ranked 22nd of 22 classes in the seventh grade.

As you traveled along the reverse evolutionary highway from 7-1 to 7-22, at each exit ramp, something was compromised – reading score, report card grades, intellect, motivation, social graces, regard for life. While disparities between consecutive or even twice removed classes could go virtually unnoticed (a reading score deviation here, a subject grade there), by the time you reached 7-22, there was such an unfathomable chasm that most students at opposite ends of the numerical class spectrum avoided each other like Romulans and Klingons.

Since members of Class 7-22 felt obliged to live up to their dubious reputation, teachers learned to abandon all faith upon entering their domain. They were like the John Travolta-led Sweathogs of *Welcome Back Kotter*, except my band of delinquents would have seen Vinny Barbarino, Freddie "Boom Boom" Washington, Juan Epstein, and their class of social misfits, as a bunch of wimps.

## A Rude Introduction

The day before I was to be officially tossed to the pre-teen and teen seventh-grade wolves, Mr. Richter decided to introduce me to my homeroom class, some of whom looked old enough to vote. I guess he figured this would lend some credibility to their finding an unfamiliar white man lurking in their room, though I would be their fourth teacher in five months.

After firing three warning shots in the air and scattering a few truants in the hallway, Mr. Richter entered the room followed by me, his reluctant protégé. He then introduced me as their new teacher, which evoked some unnerving chuckling, whispering, and – could it be – drooling? His announcement that I would be taking over for Mr. Goldberg led to more chuckling.

*What the hell happened to Goldberg?*

Once Mr. Richter described his expectations, which I was sure no one really expected, we headed for the door, returning the class to their clearly overmatched substitute teacher. The man obviously wanted no part of being there and hesitatingly followed us with a "Please take me with you" look on his face.

## The Journey Begins

The next morning, I stood by the doorway to Room 202 as my detainees staggered in to hang up their outerwear – or so I thought. As a young would-be matador held his coat like a bullfighter's cape, another intellectually misguided youth lowered his head and charged with bovine-like intent. A deft move by the matador-in-training led the rampaging seventh grader straight into the closet door.

Before I could attend to the fallen *toro* wannabe, a grinning entrepreneur – still wearing his Savage Skull jacket – held a coat in front of me, identified it as Mr. Goldberg's, and asked if I wanted to buy it.

"He'll probably be back for it," I said.

"I don't think so."

"What happened to Mr. Goldberg?"

"He had an accident. Our last three teachers all had accidents."

Another student filled in the relevant details. "Mr. Goldberg tripped over Jamal who was crawling behind him, looking for his ink pen on the floor."

Later I learned that Morris Goldberg was last seen dashing to the nearest exit, babbling incoherently and threatening to return to combat duty overseas, "where you were allowed to carry a gun." At least this put an end to the nagging question of, "Where's Goldberg?"

Once the coats were as hung up as they were going to be, I opened the roll book Mr. Goldberg would surely never need again and took attendance:

"Juan Alvarez?"

Voice: "Yo, here."

"Tyrone Bell?"

Voice: "Yeah."

"Catalino Cintron?"

Voice 1: "He's in Juvenile Court."

Voice 2: "He didn't do it."

Voice 3: "Yo mama did it."

Just then the bell rang, signaling the start of the first period. So much for attendance. As the Legion of Doom filed out and assumed their positions throughout the building, I muttered a feeble "dismissed" and looked at my teaching schedule. This was a professional prep period for me. What the hell was I going to prep?

## An "Adapted" Curriculum

I remembered I was supposed to "adapt the curriculum to meet the students' needs."

What could I possibly teach Class 7-22 that they might find useful in their daily (or future) lives? I spent many long hours trying to "adapt the curriculum." Here's the best I could come up with:

* How to Write a Letter of Confession

Use specific language in stating the nature of your crime. Focus on the crime you are currently accused of. Do not mention crimes that have so far gone undetected. Include a hint of remorse. Use phrases like "sincerely regret," "now realize," "promise to never again."

Don't complain about how you messed up or discuss

what's going to happen to whoever ratted on you.

\* How to Punctuate a Ransom Note

In the unlikely event you need to notify someone that you have found yourself in unlawful possession of his/her relative or friend, your correctly punctuated note should read: "Follow these directions and no one will get hurt: (colon)...If you want to see Waldo again, (comma)..."

\* How to Plea Bargain

Review sample scenarios: "If Roman is busted for carrying three kilos of cocaine, how much time will he serve if he tells the D.A. who wasted Julio last December?"

\* How to Behave in Family Court

Be sure to hang out with the right family.

Do not disturb or threaten any other family.

Address the judge as "Your Honor," not "Yo Judge" or "My Brother."

\* How to Qualify for Early Parole

Check Morgan Freeman's "repentant" speech before the parole board in *The Shawshank Redemption*. Remember it took him forty years to get it right.

## Surviving the Spring Semester

Somehow I survived my initiation period, which was, mercifully, only half a year. I passed most of their tests; they failed most of mine. It was definitely a case of learning under fire (not literally – thankfully), but somewhere along the way, once my classes got the idea I wasn't going to leave, we reached a tenuous détente. It was kind of an unspoken agreement that if I returned each day, refused to crumble, and continued trying to impersonate an educator, they would agree to let me live.

## Lessons Learned

Those first five months taught me a few things:
* Never Let Them See You Sweat

Look like you know what you're doing. Don't project jittery nerves or indecision. My first day, Mr. Richter visited me shortly after I had exposed my unprotected flank to the mercy of one of my classes. I innocently asked my supervisor if I should open a window. He turned his back to the class, and, scarcely moving his lips, mouthed, "Open it, shut it, or leave it alone. Just do it like you mean it!"

This seemingly innocuous piece of advice stayed with me for decades: Just open it, shut it, or leave it alone.
* Don't Bullshit Them

If you step on a textbook or on a misplaced weapon and fall on your ass, don't think you can jump up and claim to be demonstrating the Law of Gravity. Give your audience some credit. They may not know a verb from a fish, but they've been around the block.
* Size Doesn't Matter

I've seen massive body-builders reduced to gelatinous masses (Goldberg was a burly 6' 2"), and pint–sized apparent "sacrificial lambs" whose classes ran like well-oiled machines. Armed police, hoping to scare kids into socially acceptable behavior, returned with unnerving tales of having to duck to avoid flying objects, while Miss Cully, a petite and attractive third-year teacher, enjoyed impeccable classroom control.

This could be an urban legend, but as the story goes – on her first day, facing a class of eighth graders who sent their high school applications directly to Attica (Why do they do that to us novices?) the boys stood up on cue, dropped their pants, and stared at Miss Cully, waiting for her to scream, faint, or flee the scene. Instead, Miss Cully returned their stare and, in an even tone, said, "I've seen better." Her antagonists sheepishly lifted their pants and returned to their seats.

* Use the Big Bang Theory

As explained to me by a veteran teacher, if you create a loud, unexpected noise (slamming a book, knocking over a chair, etc.) there will be an immediate, but brief, moment of dead silence. For that instant, you will have everyone's attention – and you'd better have something damn good to say. You won't get a second chance.

* Be Prepared for the Jeckyll & Hyde Syndrome

Your students will not be the same people before and after lunch. Following a "healthy" dose of New York City Board of Education cuisine (as served in the '70s, '80s, and '90s), even your best-behaved or semi-comatose pupils will become crazed sugar junkies. It's your job to channel that newfound burst of energy into something resembling productive behavior, while holding casualties to a minimum.

* Know Which Words to Avoid When Teaching Rhyme

Pity the poor inexperienced fool who asks for a rhyme word for "duck," "mitts," "sick," or "runt." Don't give them the opportunity to rally around a cause célèbre. They'll find enough grist for their feverish little mills on their own.

* Have Some Friends in the Class

While you shouldn't suck up to your students – they're more perceptive than you think – try not to alienate the entire class. This will lessen the chances of a full-blown mutiny. It will also increase the probability of you reaching your car safely in the p.m.

## Park at Your Own Risk

A fledgling teacher's education also takes place outside the classroom. Even something as routine as parking the car can be a learning experience. At first, parking on the school block seemed like a good idea to me, due to the steady activity – the constant ebb and flow – around the school. Staff went out for lunch, visitors entered (hopefully unarmed), police removed selected students for questioning – mostly honor students ("Yes, Your Honor"). And, of course, there was always the welcome convenience of a speedy getaway after dismissal.

Proximity parking made perfect sense until the day, about two weeks into my tenure, when I dove into my car at three o'clock, turned the key, and – nothing. Turning the key over again and again only served to reproduce the eerie sounds of silence. When I looked under the hood, I noticed an ominously empty space where my car's battery once sat – securely bolted to its pan.

Another teacher, observing my plight, directed me to the gas station on the corner to buy back my battery. "They'll even install it at no charge," he said.

"You're kidding!"

"It's the law of the jungle. Everybody profits."

"How the hell does everybody profit? I'm paying twice for the same battery!"

"You profit by learning not to park on this street."

"So where am I supposed to park?"

"On some other street."

"Is that safe?"

"Safe? You want safe, park in Riverdale" (a relatively unthreatening neighborhood on the outskirts of The Bronx).

Determined to withdraw my unintended support for the South Bronx's version of free enterprise, the next day I arrived early and surveyed the neighborhood until I discovered a block with a church and just two parked cars. I left my beat up Rambler Classic behind the sleek vehicle nearest the church, assuming it belonged to the monsignor or some other religious official, locked my car, and began walking away, secure in the belief that parking in front of a house of worship was as good as it gets.

Glancing back, I noticed a hand-written sign in the window of the car parked in front of mine. *Probably a benediction*, I mused. As I reversed my field and approached the car, the writing became clear: "If you park me in I will keel you."

I immediately decided I might be better off parking somewhere else. But where was this mythical place called "somewhere else"? Eventually I found another parking spot near a busy intersection about two blocks further from the school, with no visible threats attached to any of the parked cars. Just another learning experience for the new educator in town.

## I Gotta Be Me

In the years that followed, in addition to becoming an accomplished valet parker, I grew more confident of my classroom technique. Being as structured as a drug-induced cattle stampede, I depended less on detailed lesson plans and more on the spontaneity that seemed better suited to my personality. (I also felt better suited to going suitless, thereby predating "Casual Friday" by a full two decades, while extending the practice to the entire workweek.)

This is not to suggest I evolved into a casually dressed, uninspired classroom entertainer. I was just a guy comfortable with his material, who sketched a rough outline, wrote a few samples or guide questions on the board, and then did forty-five minutes of standup – keeping it relaxed, spontaneous, and sprinkled with humor. I also relied on original and modified word games as reinforcement. Ultimately my audience got its money's worth. (I know it was free education, but it was worth every cent.)

Sometimes a student would ask a question or make a

comment that sent me off in a different direction. If I liked it, I'd go with it. (Hey, if Nunzio came up with a better lesson than mine...) But somehow, by the end of the class, I usually managed to tie it all together.

Passersby could always tell when I was doing a mandatory, State-required official observation lesson by the exasperated look on the face of the mandatory official observer seated in the back of the room, desperately trying to follow the official lesson plan I had handed her and discarded about two minutes into the period.

## All Classes Are Not Created Equal

Of course, my "Heeere's Johnny!" approach wasn't appropriate for all classes. It's not a one-size-fits–all world and this was definitely not a one-size-fits-all school. While experience removed the "raw meat" tag from around my neck, I was not immune to those classes who made it clear they were being detained against their will. With no ostensible concern for literature, grammar, punctuation, life, liberty – or the pursuit of anything legal, educational, social, or painless – they had to be approached differently. My job was clearly to get as many as possible out of the room unscathed.

These young academicians saw any instructional setting as the perfect venue for settling unresolved differences of opinion, and, left to their own devices, would turn each class into a UFC Steel Cage Match. Here, student-teacher interaction had to be modified. For these classes, I found an untapped capacity for structure, much like a condemned man finds religion. The plan (depending on the degree of potential rowdiness) included copying, reading, writing, handing it in, getting it back. Little discussion, limited student/teacher interaction, no lively intra-class conversation. No excuse to turn my classroom into a steel cage.

## And His Name Was Raphael

Sometimes all it took was one student to light a fuse that would detonate an entire class – and his name was Raphael.

Raphael was somewhat bigger than his classmates (and most of his teachers) probably due, at least in part, to his having spent nearly two presidential administrations in the eighth grade. He didn't speak much, except for an occasional "Fee-fi-fo-fum." Fortunately, Raphael usually showed up drowsy, after a hard night of pillaging and plundering. Raphael taught me that there were times when sleeping in class should not only be tolerated, it should be encouraged.

"Look, Mr. B. Raphael is sleeping."

"Yes, and if we keep it quiet, he'll stay that way. Anyone who wakes him will answer to me!"

I knew the lad must have been exhausted from a long night of redistributing his neighbors' assets, and so, although Raphael might not have reaped the benefits of a free education, while he slept, he wasn't terrorizing the community or the school, or threatening to eat his classmates. Raphael may not have learned how to diagram a sentence or conjugate a verb, but the class, and perhaps much of the South Bronx, was better served for the forty-five minutes each day he lay unconscious in my room.

## *Et Tu*, Victor?

Since I encouraged lively discussion in most of my classes, it generally helped to have my students fully conscious. Therefore, while Raphael was allowed to rejuvenate his body by catching up on his much-needed rest, I found it disturbing that Victor, in another class, nodded off regularly, often in the middle of some of my best material.

I spoke to the youngster, asking all the required, politically correct, pedagogical questions: "Are you getting enough sleep? Are you feeling well? Are you bored with the work we're doing in class? Is your daddy growing funny plants in the backyard?"

When I didn't get any helpful answers, I called Victor's home and spoke to his mother. I soon discovered she was proficient in several languages. Unfortunately, English wasn't one of them. Having taken Spanish in high school, I decided to give it a try. Somehow, despite my best efforts, I managed to convince Mrs. Torres that I had killed her son. By the time the screaming had turned to mournful sobs, I recalled the word for sleeps: "*Duerme! Duerme!*" I shouted. *"Victor duerme en mi clase!"*

Once the revised message registered, Mrs. Torres managed to convey that Mr. Torres would see me the following morning at eight o'clock, before he went to work. This was a full hour before my first class, but, fearful of inadvertently threatening to annihilate the remaining members of her family, and having by now lost all confidence in my ability to communicate in any language but my own, I accepted her vaguely comprehensible proposal, desperately hoping for a more productive discussion with Dad.

The next day, Mr. Torres arrived at eight-thirty, and, to my relief, presented a slight upgrade in communication as we managed to combine English and Spanish into a reasonably intelligible exchange. He requested permission to observe his son, who was (thankfully) in my first period class. Reluctant to rekindle another linguistic mishap, I agreed to let him observe his child from the back of the room.

My lesson on communication skills (purely a coincidence) went very well. Victor stayed awake for the entire performance, even raising his hand in response to a question that had been asked and answered five minutes earlier. I was obviously wasting this good man's time.

All of a sudden, there was a resounding thud from the back

of the room. All eyes were on Mr. Torres, who had apparently dozed off, fallen from his chair, and landed rather conspicuously on the floor. (Are you kidding me?)

## The Problem Is A-Parent

Official parent-teacher conferences were held in the afternoon and early evening twice a year and generally proceeded without any major problems. An irate parent here, an intimidated novice teacher there – nothing more.

I welcomed the chance to "Meet the Parents" and our discussions were usually interesting, respectful, and productive. Some parents – or guardians or friends of the family or estranged "uncles" – came to hear what I had to say about their children's classroom performances.

Some came to apologize. Some came for advice as they helplessly groped for answers. *Ever think of whacking the little...?* Some came because they got lost on their way to the all-night buffet. Still others came to flex their muscles.

Some flexed in the hallway. They would fight over their place in line as if they were waiting to be served at the local supermarket's deli counter:

"You left. You lost your place in the line!"

"I went to the bathroom!"

"You went to check the other lines!"

"You calling me a liar?"

*Children, children!*

One year the school decided to give out numbers. Another year they tried sign-in sheets. Same results, maybe worse.

### Staying flexible

Others – or perhaps some of the same – came inside to flex during classroom conferences. I found them the most amusing.

*

I greeted Mrs. Cortez at the door and escorted her to a seat by my desk. Then I opened my marking book, read her Diego's test scores, and began discussing his tenuous status in my class. But Mrs. Cortez needed more. She asked to see my book so she could compare her son's grades to those of his classmates.

When I explained this would invade the privacy of other students, she leaned over my desk and reached for the marking book, intent on independent perusal. I immediately regained control of my book, and, after awarding her an Olympic "10" for speed, distance, and agility, dismissed everyone named Cortez from my room. Clearly, Diego's test scores were the least of his problems.

*

"Ah, Mr. Connor." I'd recently broken up a fight in the library between his son, Derek, and another boy. Actually, it hadn't been much of a fight. Derek was getting thoroughly pummeled. Expecting words of appreciation, I escorted the gentleman to a seat. "I'm glad to see you, Mr. Connor."

But gratitude clearly wasn't on his mind. He glared at me and growled, "I don't want you to ever put your hands on my son again!"

*What?* "No problem, sir. The next time Derek is getting the snot kicked out of him, I'll walk away."

"Well, I didn't mean..."

"Don't worry, sir. You've got my word."

"Yes, but you can...It's your job."

"No, my job is to call for assistance. I'll just send for an administrator. I'll advise my colleagues to do the same. Someone will surely arrive in five to ten minutes. They can call 911."

"All right. You can do what you have to..."

"Next!"

\*

Although student attendance at parent/teacher conferences was discouraged and the school provided marginal supervision in the auditorium, Mrs. Martinez passed on the opportunity to cut the cord for an hour or two and brought Julio into the conference with her. The parent who opted out of the auditorium accommodation usually asked for permission before arriving in the company of the accused. But I was prepared to let it go. What I wasn't prepared for was Mrs. Martinez.

"I understand you and Julio have had some problems," she began. "Well, there are two sides to every story. I'd like to hear both sides. I'm sure we'll be able to settle this."

*What? This disruptive little misfit was going to explain why he calls out, steals from other students, puts gum on their chairs, and cuts classes? And I would explain why this pisses me off?* I declined the opportunity to throw myself at the mercy of Mrs. Martinez's court.

"Let me get this straight, ma'am. Julio and I are going to present our cases and you will decide who's to blame for his anti-social behavior. Like two pre-teens, we'll compromise – try to work it out, learn how to play together? I have a better idea. Let's bring this to 'The People's Court.' Have Judge Wapner rule on it. It would make for good TV. I definitely see reality show potential here."

I never said all conferences were productive.

\*

Mrs. Ayala was a welcome sight since she hadn't returned any of my phone calls. I explained that her son liked to sit in the back of the room with pencils stuck in both ears.

Mrs. Ayala clarified the situation: "He's just itchin' his ears."

"Just itching? But he sits there all period with...Your son sticks pencils in his ears!"

"Just itchin' his ears."

It hardly paid to mention the missing homework assignments. "Next!"

\*

"Good evening, ma'am."

"I'm Mrs. Banks, Lionel's mother. I believe you're picking on Lionel because he's black."

"Lionel is black?" I wasn't about to dignify the speaker or lend credibility to her absurd allegations by defending myself against a load of croc from this misguided alligator.

"He's a good boy. He ain't never been arrested, but once."

"Yes, Mrs. Banks. We're all proud of Lionel." *Ever consider raising the bar?*

I remembered my conversation with Lionel earlier that week, when I spoke with him after class. I know I'm throwing political correctness to the wind, but we're talking about an arrogant misanthrope with virtually no redeeming qualities. Lionel was a bully and a thief, with a history of racial instigation – totally defiant of all authority. Skin color was not his issue. It was, in fact, his only non-abrasive feature. But he was apparently well taught at playing the race card.

Lionel had glared at me: "You don't like me because I'm black."

"That's ridiculous," I'd replied indignantly. "I wouldn't like you no matter what color you were."

For the first time, Lionel had been speechless, obviously expecting a more defensive response.

Now here was his mother spouting the same worn-out line. "Mrs. Banks, you might consider having Lionel take responsibility for his actions. He's given us many reasons to single him out, but the color of his skin isn't one of them." *Have you seen the class photo?*

She mellowed a bit and guardedly mentioned problems she was having with Lionel. I gave her an inordinate amount of time – no doubt making a few enemies among those not-so-patiently waiting their turn – but this was uncharted territory for Mrs. Banks and I didn't want to lose my *carpe diem* moment.

Win a few...

## We Are Assembled Here Today

When grade assemblies were held in the school auditorium, it was our job to corral the invading hordes and then get them seated and marginally attentive. Because of the diversity of classes – and teachers – we helped each other by redistributing the load. Like in football, when an offensive lineman or tight end slides over to help double-team a disruptive defensive tackle, we instinctively double-teamed – or even triple-teamed – a troublesome class and always came to the aid of any struggling colleague.

Once the troops were assembled, it was up to whoever commanded the stage not to mess it up. When this captive audience was required to focus on the principal, a strong assistant principal, or the dean of students, it made our jobs easier. On the other hand, a fumbling child in an ill-conceived talent show could negate our good intentions and reclaim all the territory we had struggled to gain.

## The Candy Man Cometh

However adept we were at taming the masses, when the Candy Man came to town, we knew it was time to abandon ship. He was our version of Crazy Eddie, the TV ad maniac of

New York City-area late '70s and '80s television who helped inspire today's frenetic commercials and infomercials.

The Candy Man's performance was actually a synthesis of Crazy Eddie ("Our prices are insane!"), *The Price Is Right* ("It's a brand new blah!"), and *Let's Make a Deal* ("Let's see what's behind Curtain Number Two!").

While, over the years, teachers learned to avoid group responses (group answers can lead to group action, which could inspire a hostile takeover), the Candy Man dove into the shark-filled waters with lines of chum dangling from both legs. From the moment this pretentious candy evangelist took the stage, the audience was hopelessly out of control. He would scream, "Candy! Candy! Candy! Sell! Sell! Sell!" and ask inflammatory questions that elicited howling responses.

Then came the payoffs: "If you sell ___ boxes of candy and if you make ___ dollars in sales, you get (curtain raised) – a new radio!...a Princess phone!...(Remember we're talking '70s and '80s here)...a walkie talkie!...a camera!...an 8-inch personal TV!...a rabid pit bull!" With each revelation, the audience's response grew louder as the Candy Man expertly whipped his fanatical followers into a frenetic feeding frenzy.

The Candy Man had the uncanny ability to end his insane spiel just as the signal sounded for the change of period. The bell tolled in eerie unison with his final question: "What are you gonna do?" followed by the manic response: "Sell! Sell! Sell!"

We didn't delude ourselves into believing we had a prayer to control the erupting tsunami and thanked our deities of choice if our next period was administrative, preparatory – anything without these revved up kids. Those of us who had to entertain any segment of these youthful capitalists recognized the futility of our tasks. In fact, some teachers feigned illness or offered financial bribes to secure last-minute replacements.

Fortunately, these pedagogical nightmares usually played

out just before lunch, so the load generally fell on a pissed-off assistant principal or an unfortunate dean. They did their best to calm the nascent entrepreneurs, but Freddy Krueger would have had a nightmarish time getting these crazed disciples seated and fed.

### Closing the deal

Somehow these young tycoons-in-training always managed to sell an unfathomable amount of candy, suggesting either they were the most persuasive salespeople on the planet (not withstanding the young lady who was offering one for the price of two) or local residents viewed their purchases as temporary insurance policies against vandalism, theft, and bodily harm.

Then there was the problem of inappropriate distribution of goods. Sixth graders generally needed at least one eighth-grade "buddy" or an adult relative waiting in a car outside the school to prevent a misappropriation of the boxed sweets. No matter how it unfolded, by the time the candy was distributed and consumed, there probably wasn't a healthy tooth in the neighborhood.

### Just a suggestion

I suggested that the Candy Man's demonic approach to mass hysteria could be used as positive motivation. How about an assembly program turning the reluctantly assembled masses into a hysterical mob over job possibilities available to the well educated? "You can be a doctor! A lawyer! An Indian chief! OK – now: STUDY!"

## There's No Substitute

Not surprisingly, finding substitute teachers willing to suffer the slings and arrows of outrageous students in the South

Bronx was a daunting task. In my school, trolling for subs was like fishing with cardboard. Even teachers who were financially destitute or chronically unemployed routinely rejected the opportunity to expose themselves to these young vultures seeking new carrion. Therefore the regular staff was often called upon to "cover" a class for an absent colleague.

## No giving her the slip

The dreaded "coverage slips" were written and distributed each morning in the main office by Mrs. Kalb, a pint-sized automaton, who, without looking up, had an uncanny ability to sense your presence. Although many tried fleeing the office immediately after punching in and emptying their mailboxes, even the most seasoned veterans were often unable to duck a coverage.

We learned not to argue with the unflappable Mrs. Kalb. Staying on her good side was imperative since she had the authority to hand out coverages like parking tickets. Whether you got Class 6-2 in the morning or 8-20 just after lunch depended on the whim of this modern-day Queen of Hearts. Engaging Mrs. Kalb in pleasant conversation was just another exercise in futility, since the chat would inevitably conclude with you being handed a coverage slip, albeit with a fabricated smile.

## "Catch me if you can."

The ultimate "duck" was attempted by Dante Volga, who relished his coverages like a salmon delights in attending grizzly bear luncheons. One day, Mr. Volga didn't show up for his assignment. The loudspeaker blared: "Mr. Volga! Class 8-16 is waiting for you in Room 319!"

The next thing I knew, there was Mr. Volga slipping into my room. After a quick glance over his shoulder, he silently slithered along the wall like Spiderman. As the sound of approaching footsteps were heard mounting the stairs, the runaway educator faced my class, holding a finger to his lips.

The class, recognizing a fugitive, remained silent. As the footsteps grew louder, Mr. Volga dove to the floor and hid behind a full-bodied student in the rear of the room. Just then, the principal appeared at my door.

"Have you seen Mr. Volga?" he asked.

I shook my head and the class, not about to give him up, offered no clue to the intruder's whereabouts.

Soon a new announcement blared: "Mr. Rizzo! Please cover Class 8-16 in Room 319, immediately!" My class cheered in boisterous tribute to the one that got away.

**"I've got you covered."**

Armed with composition paper, word games, and puzzles, I covered my share of orphaned classes. These unsolicited assignments were, for the most part, forgettable. However, one coverage was memorable.

I was assigned an absent colleague's eighth grade English class. As my temporary charges worked on word puzzle sheets, I noticed a crude statue of Shakespeare in the back of the room. "Are you reading Shakespeare?" I asked the puzzle solvers in the first row.

"Yes, we just started last week," a helpful voice volunteered.

"Which one?" I continued.

"William."

*I should have known.*

## Calling Mrs. Wilkes!

Most coverages were for daily absences. However, if a staff member required extended leave, a long-term substitute had to be recruited. This pedagogical crusader had to be willing to undergo his/her own lengthy "Goldberg experience." Fortunately, there was always Mrs. Wilkes – a short, stocky, middle-aged Afro-American – whose utter lack of teaching skills was rivaled only by her uncanny ability to antagonize everyone.

Mrs. Wilkes made no effort to conceal her contempt for the entire student population. In fact, the only things she inspired in her classes were the Three Rs – resentment, rebellion, and retribution. However, Mrs. Wilkes was no Goldberg. She took her young adversaries' best shots and kept coming back for more. No amount of abuse would deter her from her self-determined mission - whatever the hell that was.

This woman could transform the most docile, even-tempered, educationally oriented, well-grounded students into a riotous horde. But, for all her negatives, Mrs. Wilkes had one redeeming attribute that dwarfed her limitless limitations: She was available.

So when I broke my ankle in 1990, the call went out for the imperturbable, the impenetrable, the implacable, the ever-available Mrs. Wilkes. For seven weeks, she held my classes in dubious sway. They were exposed to her whims and machinations – and she was exposed to theirs.

## I Have Returned!

When I finally limped back to school – using a single crutch – my classes were surprisingly excited to see me and I was actually happy to be there. ("Happy" may be too strong a word. I welcomed the opportunity...I looked forward to...I knew the time was right...I was fed up with sitting on my ass.)

However, when I returned to the classroom, I realized I had never given a thought to what I'd actually do the day I resumed my career. Though my daily lessons were no models of structural perfection, I always (usually?) had some semblance of a plan.

But that day I had nothing – *nada*, not a clue. I had no idea of what they'd learned during my absence, and no clear recollection of what I had started, completed, or intended to teach. Any notes and other materials I had left on my desk were long gone. So I resorted to the shamelessly banal: I had my classes write compositions about what happened during my absence.

The results were eye-opening, unexpected, and blatantly unfiltered accounts of the previous weeks' activities. I retained the compositions, realizing that neither they, nor the events they "commemorated," would be easily replaced.

Some excerpts follow, unedited for grammar, spelling or style, though I felt compelled to alter names and diffuse a few f-bombs. Levels of written expression and degrees of indignation and retaliation reflect the makeup of the various classes. But even the casual reader will discern a common thread.

## You Can't Make This Stuff Up. (OK, maybe you can, but I didn't.)

"First we were glad you were gone but then we were sorry."
*Thank you, I think.*

"During the past few weeks we had a sub from Hell! She has lots of Rinkel's on her. And she has a big gray wig and a wart like a frog. And big Rocket lanchers. She has big pimples and a big head and a mustash."

*We've spoken about not judging people on the surface. Shame on you!*

"She bearly fit at the desk when she sat down the desk was at least three feet away."

*Really?*

"Sometimes she would walk around to check work and accidently poke people with her humugus rochets and I got hit in the head with those rochets. When she bent over she knocked me out of my chair."

*Got you coming and going, huh?*

"...made us walk around her so we were late to class."

*That may be a bit of a stretch.*

"She had fake busams because when she hit me with them they shifted to the side of her."

"She smelled like dirty pampers and A jacks."

"I think she does'nt take a bath. Because she smells like shit! Her armpits stink like hell."

*We could have a personal hygiene issue here.*

"She farts when she washes the board with her filthy old spung."

"She told us we are stinck people."

*Sometimes it's hard to access blame when standing in the eye of a fart.*

"Then she pulled me and christie to the side a told us to stop hangout with Benny because she said he was a dick."

*Sounds like an inappropriate attempt at counseling.*

"Mrs. Wilke told the whole class even the good people mental retarted class. She called vanessa and christie a f____n' bitch and they walked out of the classroom."

*Now we seem to be moving beyond a few extra pounds, facial hair, and personal hygiene.*

"She cursed at us and said people like us caused all the troubles in the world we made diseases and poor neighborhood."

*We're gonna need some damage control here.*

"she gets everbody in trouble, she marks people cutting when they are absent, she takes attendence all period and she takes attendance after school so we are late for the bus."

*I sense administrative potential.*

"She write referrals for no reason. I bet half the forest and rain forest in the world was cut down to supply her referals. She sits on her fat ass and writes referals and police reports and she doesnt even look up."

*Definite administrative possibilities here.*

"Mrs. Wilkes also said that you were a pig. And when we use to ask her where you were she would say I don't know and I don't care with a snodoo attitude."

*You've invented a new word. Now I'm a pig? This is getting personal.*

"So I said to Angela I miss Mr. berliner then she said I hope that stupid teacher doesnt come back."

*I never even met the woman.*

"One day she took everything out of the draws and threw your stuff off the desk and made us shove it in the closet."

*Hey, that's my stuff!*

## And the hits just keep on coming:

"She is always saying ASS."

*Like how?*

"She told tacheldia to sit her fart ass down on the chair."

*Oh, I see.*

"And she accussed Axina, shawette, me, and other people of robbing her. Now we all have to go back to court on May, 22. But until this date we are on probation for the police."

*Some serious shit.*

"I told her to go f___ herself."

*Can't really condone this, but the defense appears to be unraveling.*

"And every day there was a riote. 6-7 or 6-9 through all the papers and alot of the books out the window and she did not have any controlle."

*Are those my papers?*

"And I said I miss Mr. Berliner and she said F___ you Mr. Berliner is a sthoubet Bitch. And I told her she is a sick mother f_____."

*This kid's got a few rough edges, but I'm glad he's on my side.*

"She did not teach us nothing the all time we were here."

*Didn't I teach you not to use a double negative?*

"During the 6-7 weeks i hated her. She never Didn't do nothing."

*Congratulations! You've discovered the triple negative!*

"We throw book out the window and she keep writting referals and detention papers on all of us some of us did not do nothing. Some of us did do something."

*Ya think?*

"Angela threw books and Sofia threw books. I only threw one book."

*Good for you! Probably only a paperback, right?*

"We throw books at her and we throw orange pels at her and paper airplanes at her."

"Ms Woikes As ben a F____n' night mare she as Ben geting me in troble and she says that I throw A brush and it wasent me it was dante Carter."

*Right. You threw the oranges.*

"And Miss Wilkes things she is big and bad but she is only big And Brain said something I cant tell you."

*There's more? What could you possibly be holding back?*

"She taught us the national anthem and the nigro national anthem when this is a C.A. class not music."

*How the hell did she get you to sing?*

"I'm telling you, those 7 weeks were HELL! Now, I'm glad she is gone and I don't want to see that big tity, big but, hairy thing ever, ever, ever again."

*Yes, but how do you really feel?*

To be fair – and politically correct – I will offer the lone dissenting view:

"She was OK. but she had an atitude, But she was nice enough to say to me you won't get a 75 on your report card this time. Because I was doing well."

*At what?*

"One day she was absent and we had this Indian guy with two or three teeth. He let us do what ever we want he just smiled at us. We all got in lots of trouble. Two deans broke up fights and yelled at us the hole time."

*I get it. You need me to protect you from yourselves. Next week we read* Lord of the Flies.

"So for the first time in my life, I'm actually glad you're here!"

*You damn well should be!*

"P S During the past few weeks we Realized how much you ment to us and what a good teacher you are."

*It's good to be missed, but it's a pretty low bar.*

And finally, my personal favorite:

"I know it's hard to be home in a casket."

*Did I fail to mention it was just a broken ankle?*

## To Be Taken Orally

One year, in their infinite wisdom, the administrative big wigs decided all students should recite oral reports to their classes. Each speaker would be required to explain a "how-to" process to his/her classmates in a two – three minute speech. The official rationale was long and vacuous, but it seemed like a good idea, especially since I found little joy in marking papers and welcomed the opportunity to discuss the art of public speaking.

However, I had reservations about oral reports in classes

where speaking was necessarily restricted, realizing some urchins might not benefit academically or otherwise from enhanced freedom of expression. But I had a relatively decent mix of classes that year, so I decided to give oral reports a try.

### ¿*Que pasa*, Carlos?

My concerns were validated the day Carlos, a previously reticent lad, took the podium. I had one eye on Carlos and one eye on the rest of the class as I tried to follow the boy's fractured English. I was proud of him for making the attempt, until I realized this newly-emboldened public speaker was giving a treatise on how to make progress with a girl.

Once I saw where he was going with his report, and envisioned my career swirling rapidly down the drain, I told the aspiring orator to return to his seat. After thanking Carlos for his efforts (questionable as they were), I announced to the class that all future oral reports would be submitted in writing. This reinforced my notion that for certain classes, to ensure classroom tranquility, First Amendment rights should be constructively amended.

## The Standards

As we approached the 21st century, the Board of Regents, in its never-ending pursuit of bureaucratic time consumption for the sole purpose of justifying its tenuous existence, created a code of "Performance Standards" for New York State students. Scores of pencil pushers, most of whom hadn't seen the inside of a classroom since their college days, devised a convoluted list of objectives ranging from the glaringly obvious ("Read to improve reading skills") to empty – "What you talkin' 'bout Willis?" – inanities ("Use previous experience to respond to a diversity of influential blah, blah, blah...").

We were all given overviews of the Performance Standards

for our middle school subject areas, along with explicit instructions to hang them on the wall, use them as lesson plan guidelines, and refer to them often. I hung them on the wall.

## Standards of Relief

One day, when using the third floor facilities, I noticed a new poster over the second urinal from the right. A creative colleague from the Industrial Arts Department had expanded the Standards to cover experiences outside the classroom. I have always been impressed with its eerie likeness to the state-mandated code:

### MIDDLE SCHOOL BATHROOM STANDARDS

OVERVIEW OF THE PERFORMANCE STANDARDS

B    BATHROOM

B1   BATHROOM PROCEDURES

B1a Unlock door.

B1b Choose bowl or urinal.

B1c Wash and/or use towel.

B2   BATHROOM DECISIONS

B2a Unzip or pull down pants.

B2b Cover seat or lift to 90 degrees.

B2c Open or close windows.

B2d Wiggle or drip dry.

B3   BATHROOM THINKING

B3a Use previous experience to identify bowl and urinal.

B3b Work individually and in teams to collect and share information.

B3c Wipe in one direction (front to back or back to front).

B3d Use hand, socks or paper (if available).

B4   BATHROOM TECHNOLOGIES

B4a Use technology tools to observe and measure objects,

organisms and phenomena.

B4b Acquire information from multiple sources, e.g. newspapers, books, magazines.

B4c Recognize and record evidence of bias in data. (Make notations with free hand.)

B5  BATHROOM COMMUNICATION

B5a Argue from evidence.

B5b Critique published materials (on or off bowl).

## The Intimidator

Shortly after the invasion of the Standards, we were favored by a visit from the District Superintendent, a short humorless man, and his acolyte assistant, a gangly pompous sycophant whose nose couldn't have been any browner if he'd sniffed out a pasture of cow manure. Ostensibly at our school to observe how the Standards were being utilized, they strutted from class to class hell-bent on intimidation.

At one point, the Assistant District Superintendent asked a socially-challenged youngster how his education was progressing. The lad looked his interrogator in the eye and casually replied, "F____ you." The District Superintendent, accustomed to bringing his subjects to their knees, glared at the boy and scolded, "That's no way to speak to Mr. Ashford!" The child returned his glare and said, "F____ you too."

The district big shots limited the rest of their excursion to "interacting" with the staff. We never learned whether we met their singular "standards" for the Standards.

After they left the building, the Bathroom Standards poster reappeared over urinal #2 in the third floor men's room.

## Laughing Matters

The "Bathroom Standards" was just one example of how,

though vastly outnumbered and coping with pressures only an inner-city teacher could fathom, many of us retained some degree of sanity while trying to inflict an education on the befuddled masses yearning to be fuddled. Those of us who managed to survive maintained a sense of humor and refused to take ourselves too seriously.

*

One veteran teacher, upon hearing of a return visit by the District Intimidator and his resident puppet, covered a bulletin board in his classroom with photographs and drawings of various birds. The district had recently mandated that each teacher erect a "Word Wall" and his intent was to feign an honest misunderstanding – hence the "Bird Wall."

*

At a regularly scheduled faculty conference in the auditorium, the teacher in charge of the school's Reading Laboratory was asked to report on the success of the new-look, student-friendly reading materials. He began his talk by saying, "Student response appears to be quite positive – judging by the number of books stolen."

*

In the late 1970s, the editors of *Men's Health Magazine* published the results of a survey to determine the ten most stressful and least stressful jobs. Inner-city schoolteacher was awarded first place for "High-Stress Jobs," beating out policeman, fireman, and air-traffic controller. (Forest ranger headed the list for "Least Stressful.") The survey results were displayed in teachers' lounges throughout the school under banners proclaiming: "We're #1!"

*

One afternoon, our serious-minded Assistant Principal Jake Morgan was conferring with several teachers in his second-floor office. Meanwhile, a not-so-serious-minded science teacher in a third floor classroom just above, stealthily lowered a skeleton tied to a rope until it came to rest just outside Morgan's window. A colleague who was in on the practical joke, suggested Mr. Morgan turn and look outside. Somehow the innovative educator on the floor above had rigged the skeleton to a plastic tube and, when Morgan turned around, the skeleton was pissing on his window.

*

Long before the modern photo-copier, which spews out replicas by the hundreds at the push of a button, there was the cumbersome mimeograph machine. Teachers made copies by painstakingly inserting a hand-written or typed ink-imprinted page into an impossibly narrow slot on the roller, checking a few settings, as well as the highly unstable ink supply, and then cranking out duplicates by hand.

The few available machines were rarely, if ever, available at the same time since careless or mechanically-challenged teachers subjected the temperamental devices to regular abuse. One day this sign appeared in the second floor teachers' lounge above the only remaining functional machine:

# ACHTUNG!

## ALLES LOOKENPEEPERS
## UND NON-TECHNISHENS

**Dieser Wunderbar Hand-gebuilt
Computischabler ist NICHT für
Gefingerpoken und Mittengrabben.
Ist easy Schnappen der Springen-
werk, Blowenfusen und Poppen-
corken mit Spitzensparken.
Ist NICHT für Gewerken by das
Dummkopfen.
Das Rubbernecken Sightseeren
Please Keepen das Cottonpicken
Hands in das Pockets,
Relaxen und
Looken at das Blinken Lights.**

\*

Mark Flaherty could teach with the best, but that was not his claim to fame. With his cold steely eyes and deliberately slow menacing gestures, Mr. F. could intimidate the most unruly classes. At his discretion, the silence in his room was deafening.

Those who dared to test him (and in thirty-plus years, there were remarkably few) found he would follow them relentlessly to seek retribution. He'd visit their homes, their parents' places of business, their churches, their hangouts. He was rumored to hide in their cars, behind their bushes, and inside shower curtains.

One day, Flaherty rounded up two troublemakers and led them to what he thought was a vacant office, unaware that another teacher and I were there. He barely acknowledged us as he stood his captives against the wall and, maintaining his steely glare, slowly rolled up his sleeves. As the two trembling offenders were about to fall to their knees, Mr. Flaherty broke the oppressive silence by asking Victim #1 with exaggerated precision, "What's your name?"

As if on cue, my colleague and I burst into song: "Is it Mary or Sue?" (the next line of "What's Your Name?," a popular song in the 1960s). Mr. F., fighting mightily to suppress a smile, turned to us as if we were two delinquent children. We pointed to each other and, barely able to contain ourselves, slinked out of the room.

That afternoon we laughed about the incident with Flaherty, who, unbeknownst to the students, had a wonderful sense of humor and a highly contagious laugh. He later confessed that this was the closest he'd ever come to "losing it."

## It's the Principal

Not all of our school's zany moments were intended to amuse. In this institution of hired learning, incidental humor started at the top. Our fearless leader was a well-intentioned administrator who encouraged students and supported teachers wherever possible. However, he often left his verbal censors on hold.

\*

Once a local TV station sent a reporter and cameraman to our school to interview Principal Davis. After greeting his guests, Old Fearless sat in his new office chair, which was apparently too low, and he turned on Mr. Richter: "Dammit, Richter! What the hell kind of shitty chair are you giving me?" Fortunately, this was before the camera started filming; unfortunately, it was also before the public address system had been turned off.

*

One day we heard the familiar sound of five bells ringing three times in succession, signaling a fire drill. These drills were routine and, except for occasional attempts at insurrection, generally proceeded without serious incident.

This time however, a small smoky fire had been detected in the supply room. Principal Davis, who usually reinforced a drill with verbal instructions over the loudspeaker, began yelling, "This is not a drill! Get them out of the damn rooms!" Somehow, we pulled it off with no reported casualties.

## Humor With "Class"

Classroom humor was spontaneous and unpredictable.

*

The girl who wouldn't take "no" for an answer:

I always respected a student's need to attend to nature's call, having been embarrassed as a child by a teacher who clearly didn't. Therefore, I was generally more lenient than most in issuing bathroom passes. However, one day I sensed an unusual demand for toilet privileges and suspended the exodus, deciding to let the wooden room pass "sit" and dry off for the rest of the period.

Just after my announcement, a girl in the front row began

waving her hand. "I have to leave the room," she pleaded.

"I just said that was all for now," I reminded her.

I went back to writing on the board, but sensed that I was not alone. Little Amanda stood beside me, pulling my shirt in an effort to get my attention.

"I really have to go, Mr. Berliner."

Then in a low voice, Amanda confided: "I'm having my ministration period."

*Too much information!* I didn't even know she was a ministrator. (I wrote her an "emergency pass.")

*

The boy who wouldn't take "C" for an answer:

One afternoon, we were going over a practice reading test. Since the class was having a hard time finding the answer to a question, I explained the technique of multiple-choice elimination, telling students that, if they couldn't decide on the right answer, they should try to eliminate wrong choices.

"If you can remove one choice, your guess is one out of three," I said, explaining it was a better percentage than one of four. "If you remove two, it's 50 – 50." Together we were able to eliminate choices A, B, and D. "So the correct answer is C. Now let's look at..."

Immediately, Tyrone's hand shot up – never a good sign. "Could you give us a hint?"

"You don't need a hint. The answer is C."

"Could you narrow it down to two?"

"I narrowed it down to one. The answer is C."

"But..."

"Write C!"

*

Me: "Who fought in the Spanish-American War?"

Voice 1: "The Japanese, the French, and the Italians."
Me: "Good answer, but..."
Voice 2: "Aw, he guessed."

*

After I made a reference to the Revolutionary War:
"Did we win?"
I decided to play along with this history buff: "Well, we fought England. If we didn't win, we'd all be speaking English."
"But we do speak English," he astutely observed.
"There you go."
I resisted the temptation to take the deception any further. This was well before revisionist history elbowed its way into the curriculum and I had no desire to be a forerunner. So, accustomed as I was to going off topic, I gave a condensed, but accurate account of the Revolutionary War, right down to Paul Revere's ride – Sarah Palin notwithstanding.

## Walk the Walk

Even after a good day at the office, there was no guarantee we would arrive at our cars unscathed, especially those of us who remained to teach after-school tutorial classes. When walking the mean streets alone at day's end and seeing three or four alumni approaching, you hoped your reputation preceded you. (Actually, I hoped an armored truck preceded me.)

It was always reassuring to find at least one member of the alliance who knew you, or at least remembered you – preferably fondly.

Three dialogues:

*

"Hey, Mr. Berliner! Remember me?"
"Sure." *But you were shorter, thinner, and unarmed.* "Couple of

years ago, right?"

"Yeah. Hector Cruz."

"How are you doing, Hector?"

"You failed me, man."

"You must've deserved it."

"Yeah, I did."

Hector's companion: "You a dummy. You couldn't pass shit."

"F_____ you, Marcus. Stay cool, Mr. B."

"You too, Hector." *Where the hell did I park my car?*

*

"Mr. B, you going to your car?"

(Reluctantly) "Yeah."

"What kind of car you got?"

"Broken down piece of junk. Starts most of the time." *Like I'm going to help you identify my vehicle.*

"Want me to start it for you?"

"I don't think so." *Where's the damn car?*

*

"Hey, Mr. B, want me to walk you to your car?"

"Not necessary, Carlos. How about I save you the trip and just give you my wallet here?"

"Shit. You teachers ain't got no money."

"Yeah, and we don't even get to sell candy."

"Yeah, that was cool. Made over a hundred bucks."

"Selling candy?"

"Well, you know."

"Yeah, I know. You sure about the wallet?"

"You funny, Mr. B. Stay cool."

"Stay out of trouble, Carlos." *Where's the damn...There it is - across the street!*

# Mentor This

As my years behind the desk (or seated upon it) rolled on, our school introduced a district-sanctioned mentoring program where experienced teachers were assigned to rapidly enhance the development of fledgling educators, like some kind of pedagogical Miracle Gro. I respectfully passed on the invitation to be an official mentor, but, when asked for guidance, was always available to answer questions and offer suggestions.

No doubt this mentoring process was a good idea in theory, but that's what it was all about – theory, and I was about keeping it real. Mentors were instructed to gear their sessions towards uninspired behavioral objectives, blatantly contrived motivation, inflexible structure, and ear-catching idioms we had learned in college education courses and then selectively discarded as we applied our skills to the real world of live students.

### Your attention, please

Over the years, many novices sought me out for advice that might actually help them function in the classroom. My solicited counsel generally began with Berliner's Law: Get their attention.

I'd seen too many instances where the teacher did his scripted performance while the class did – whatever it was that they were doing. Your main objective, I explained, behavioral or otherwise, starting with the first day of school, is to get them to focus on you. You could line up Socrates, Churchill, and Knute Rockne as guest lecturers, but if no one's listening, you might as well invite Daffy Duck.

### The survivor series

My admittedly unorthodox and impromptu mentoring sessions were geared towards survival techniques. I explained the "Lessons Learned" (See pages 43-44), and encouraged practical, pragmatic ways to prolong a career so the new educator would have the opportunity to actually try out his or her damn theories. Live to teach another day.

This pragmatic approach was especially relevant as the turn of the century hastened our evolution into a litigious society, in which every student knew his/her "rights." Many potential litigants, intent on mayhem and well-schooled in creating suable situations, couldn't find page 21 after reading page 20, but they knew their "rights." I always began the year by explaining to my classes they had the right to remain silent.

Just as I insisted on my students focusing on me, I never let my focus wane. I encouraged colleagues to practice writing on the board while facing the class, to reduce, if not eliminate, the threat of spitballs, airborne pencils, or other anti-social behavior. (See book cover.)

In addition to "facing up" to their classes, I warned teachers against being left alone in the room with one or two blatant malingerers. Too many colleagues had been routinely dragged into court for improper behavior, when their only crime was allowing a potential accuser to linger in the room.

## I walk the halls

While working closely with some students could be a rewarding experience (and I certainly had my share), I recommended teacher discretion in keeping a respectable distance, especially from those with bad intentions. Over the years, many teachers had been "accidentally" blindsided. (Remember Goldberg?)

Most accidents seemed to happen when walking the crowded hallways. Some Oscar nominees would hurl themselves into the wall screaming, "He pushed me!" My advice was to always check your back (against the wall, if possible), particularly in the corridors.

Hall-walking 101 also included my personal self-preservation and professional longevity routine. When turning a corner, I advised using the arm nearest the turn to adjust your collar – or to do anything that allowed you to inconspicuously raise your forearm and use it to protect yourself from students blindly racing through the not-so-hallowed halls.

More than once I engaged a rampaging intellectual who had a reckless encounter with an unexpected forearm, then picked himself off the ground, and sheepishly apologized for the offense. I would ask if he was okay and suggest that in the future he might look where he was going.

Fortunately, there was no a hint of culpability in the forearm tactic. You were certainly not striking a defenseless student. You weren't even defending yourself, a punishable offense in this brave new litigious world. You were adjusting your collar, fixing your hair, scratching your arm, picking your nose...The suits and the suers would be hard-pressed to manufacture blame on that one.

Even women, who would never think of physically engaging a student, found merit in my "protect yourself at all times" approach. (Of course, the effectiveness of this maneuver was limited by the length and girth of the offender.) One damsel in potential distress reported back to me that she had nailed a sprinter who was pursuing his education – and Enrique Colon. Though clearly more shaken than her victim, she had enjoyed a definite sense of relief and vindication.

*

The mentoring project was abandoned after a year, with teachers demonstrating virtually no mentor-inspired improvement. However, I'd like to think there were fewer classroom uprisings and "accidental" teacher assaults. And though my approach to mentoring would never be endorsed by the reigning "suits," it's possible that over the years it saved the Board of Ed at least a few lawsuits and some teacher-leave time. Who knows?

## The Final Daze

After 33 years of tossing candles into the darkness, I knew it was time to pack it in and call it a career. The times they were a changin' and I had clearly lost a foot or two off my fastball. I could still do standup, but was relying more on worksheets and word games. I'd depleted my arsenal of mass instruction. Discipline was becoming more of an effort. I'd left it all on the field. My pension was calling; it was time to go.

I spent much of my "free" time sifting through papers that had over the years been stuffed into closets, file cabinets, and drawers. Old worksheets were relegated to trashcans; those not too badly faded, I gave away.

### Better late?

As I discarded many handfuls of long-forgotten administrative directives and memos, one pedagogical edict caught my eye. In dark print across the top, it virtually screamed: "Must be signed and submitted no later than 3:00 p.m. June 11 – absolutely no exceptions, subject to penalty of district discipline." The paper was dated June 7, 1976.

I considered handing it in that day. I could have it signed and submitted before 3:00; it would just be about twenty-five years tardy. I finally decided to add it to the overflowing trash heap since the administrator who had issued the malignant missive had long since taken his administrative, as well as his earthly leave, regretfully without ever having received my response to his urgent administrative request.

## Then in walked...

One day, while I was busy cleaning out my room, removing every last trace of my existence, in walked Cordoño, the current *Numero Uno* in the school and celebrated neighborhood "bad boy." He was a more outgoing, more personable version of Raphael, some twenty years later. I know he had personally threatened to "take out" all of his teachers and several administrators.

"You leaving?" he asked as he surveyed my room.

"Yep."

"I was hoping you'd be here until I graduate."

"Life is short," I explained.

"I'll never forget you, Mr. B."

(I'm sure he'd said this to other teachers who'd immediately notified the authorities.)

"You were the coolest teacher I ever had."

I was, in fact, his only teacher who hadn't taken out an Order of Protection against him. Cordoño knew I didn't approve of his extra-curricular activities, but as my student, he had played by my rules – more or less.

He wandered the halls like Ulysses, searching for a safe haven and usually came to rest outside my room, probably seeing this as the stopover where he stood the least chance of being arrested. He stayed out of the class' view, undoubtedly catching his breath before his next conflict.

In addition to being a local terrorist, Cordoño was actually a gifted artist. He'd occasionally given me pictures he'd drawn and asked me to take them home for my kids and to put one on my door. I had no problem accommodating him.

I'd encouraged him to pursue his one socially acceptable talent, but he seemed embarrassed by any endeavor that wasn't criminal. He pretended not to care, but maybe he had been listening.

Cordoño extended his hand; I grasped it, and we wished each other well. I never saw or heard of him again, until one day I read a small story buried in the middle of the newspaper. He would have been twenty-one-years-old.

## Did I Accidentally Get It Right?

As I think back, I suspect I must have done something right. My students were generally respectful, usually aced their reading tests, and more than a few returned to see me, some as parents – and some as grandparents (Ouch!) – of my then current students. I've even received a smattering of letters from prison assuring me, "It's not your fault." There were, remarkably, very few threats.

I've heard it said: "Those who can, do; those who can't, teach." I prefer to believe those who can do, teach.

It was one helluva ride!

# THE NOT-SO-FINE ART OF COMMUNICATION

# CAN WE TALK?

"Don't speak unless you can improve upon the silence."
– Aristotle

**I don't want to come off** as some old fart thumbing his nose at succeeding (if not actually succeeding) generations, but we seem to have evolved into a society of flagrant yakkers, anxious to speak and reluctant to listen.

## Talk Is Cheap

Somehow we've generated generations of uninspired talkers who prefer to lace their sentences with filler expressions like "you know" and "stuff like that" rather than submit a complete thought. We've managed to turn conversation into a perverted challenge to see who can talk the longest without saying anything – you know?

And then we like add to the hollow mix. "Like," a trite reminder of the hippie 1960s (ala Maynard G. Krebbs – for those who remember TV's *The Dobie Gillis Show*) has reemerged from the 1970s when it was a mainstay of the often-ridiculed "Valley Girl" dialect of suburban California.

I actually heard this: "Yeah, well, like you know, it was like wow, so like what's that about?"

*What the hell did you just say?*

## What's Your Sign?

Notice how sign language has nudged its way into our lexicon, stealthily transferring the burden of communication from speaker to listener? We've even invented air quotes – using fingers to suggest quotation marks.

We use air quotes around clichés: "I like to think of myself as a 'jack of all trades'" (air quotes around "jack of all trades") or to suggest sarcasm: "So he 'rushed over' to my house" (air quotes around "rushed over").

*

I'm reminded of Victor Borge's hilarious phonetic punctuation. Perhaps, in addition to air quotes, we should make little clicking sounds to imitate written punctuation. However, I'm also reminded of the difference between humorous and pretentious.

*

Someone please tell me why we need to pantomime references to a telephone conversation. This waste of time and energy consists of spreading the thumb and pinky while fisting the other fingers and holding what used to look like a hand next to your ear so body language can reinforce verbal expression just in case, "I'll give you a call," "Call me," or "I was just about to call Fred" didn't convey the idea of using a telephone.

Here's a thought: What if you want to air quote something related to your phone conversation while making the telephone hand gesture? You could break your damn fingers or poke out an eye.

Conversation is devolving into a pathetic game of charades, without the fun and excitement of competitive guessing: "So I typed this letter..." (gesture of typing), "I cut out a picture of..." (gesture of scissor cutting), "I had sex with..."

(Never mind).

Will we someday pantomime entire conversations? Do we have so little confidence in our ability to verbally communicate ideas? Will a mime like Marcel Marceau eventually be our Spokesman of the Year?

## The Queen of Clichés

Language mismanagement is not confined to the young. My wife has a very old (as in long-time) friend (I'll call her Lois) who, to the best of my knowledge, has yet to express an original thought. Instead, she relies on a virtual armada of clichés, which she deploys to navigate her way through every conversation.

Lois has the uncanny ability to produce a cliché on any subject – and for any occasion. She can recite a cliché to cheer you up ("Time heals all wounds"), to put you down ("He got his just desserts"), to explain ("The acorn doesn't fall far from the tree"), to rationalize ("Better late than never"), and on and on.

In Lois' world, people don't disagree; they "fail to see eye to eye." They don't work hard; they "burn the candle at both ends." When she is on her game, Lois will hit you with the double-barreled cliché: "When push comes to shove, it's sink or swim."

*Help!*

Recently, Lois' daughter, after years of "beating the bushes," finally met the "apple of her eye." Not surprisingly, he's "good as gold," "straight as an arrow," and "honest as the day is long." Lois hopes Allison doesn't let this one "slip through her fingers." (I was tempted to remind her, "You can't judge a book by its cover," but was afraid to "open a can of worms.")

When I hear a sports interview, I think of Lois since most athletes respond to reporters' questions with stock answers – or clichés. I muse over how Lois has let the opportunity of a lifetime "sail by" as I fantasize about her interviewing a sports figure:

Lois: "Your pitcher had them eating out of his hand. Then the wheels fell off. How do you get back on track?"

Baseball Player: "We're just gonna play it one game at a time."

Lois: "When you trailed by eleven runs in the eighth inning, was the team ready to throw in the towel?"

BP: "There's no quit in this team. We kept our heads in the game."

Lois: "Will you have to carry the team on your back?"

BP: "I always give 110% - but we all have to step it up. Ain't no 'I' in 'team.'"

Lois: "Yes, one for all and all for one."

BP: "Ain't no 'me' in 'team.'"

Lois: "Just pick each other up. United we stand, that's what..."

BP: "Ain't no 'w' in 'team.'"

Lois: "So you'll rally the troops and..."

BP: "Ain't no 'j' in 'team.'"

Lois: "OK, but wouldn't you say you were a dark horse?"

BP: " Ain't no...A what? Hey, who you...?"

Lois: "I mean, you have your work cut out for you. You don't want to feel the season slipping away."

BP: "We just gotta play our A-game. It ain't over till the fat lady sings."

Lois: "The bottom line is, it's not whether you win or lose, it's how you play the game."

BP: "Whatever."

I remember once at a dinner party, after a barrage of insufferable clichés (How does she remember them all?) I finally cracked and vented my frustration with a blatant cliché of my own – a non sequitur that obviously had nothing to do with anything she or anyone else had said. "I guess, you can lead a horse to water..." I announced as the other dinner guests stared in uneasy silence, recognizing my thinly veiled attempt at retaliation. Not only was the sarcasm lost on Lois, she enthusiastically completed the damn cliché!

## Substitute Words and Expressions

When did "I said" become "I went" and "she said" morph into "she goes"? And do we really need to narrate both sides of a conversation?

"So I went...and she goes...then I go..." and stuff like that.

Sometimes the speaker will conjure up that re-emergent staple "like" and give it a modern twist. So instead of "I went" and "she goes," the narrative proceeds: "I'm like, 'What are you doing?' and she's like, 'I'm totally loving this.'"

We've substituted a word for our substitute words! Not only have we fallen back in love with our precious "like" fetish, we've found a new way to use our old verbal crutch. It's like – enough!

*

What's wrong with "You're welcome" as a response to "Thank you"? Now the response of choice is "No problem." I'm not saying this New Age catch-phrase doesn't work. It can, at certain times, be a fitting rejoinder. But more often than not, it's nothing more than another uninspired example of linguistic decay.

"No problem" suggests you've gone out of your way, relinquished or conceded something, or at least made someone's life easier. When I thank a stranger at the gym for letting me "work in" with him and he says, "No problem," that's fine. He doesn't mind sharing the equipment. If you want to respond to someone who thanks you for helping to retrieve her fallen groceries, "No problem" is – no problem.

However, this conversation makes no sense:

"I hope you're feeling better soon."

"Thank you."

"No problem."

Damn right, no problem. You didn't do anything! "You're welcome" or no response at all works very well here, thank you.

I was at a restaurant recently and, after my fourth request, the waiter finally brought bread and water. When I grudgingly thanked him, his response was, "No problem."

Yes, problem. How about an apology, you toad?

## Some Linguistic Acrobatics

Why would anyone precede an explanation by announcing, "I'm not going to lie"? Does this mean you're now going into truth mode? The same goes for, "I'll be honest with you" or "I'm going to tell you the truth." What have you been doing up to now? What about people who promise to tell "the honest truth"? As opposed to what?

\*

"I'll get back to you."

Bullshit! You know you're going to have to call this putz again if you ever want to resume the conversation.

About twenty-five years ago, when I was networking for additional freelance writing, I decided to call my first publisher. After a short but pleasant conversation, he explained, "I know what it's like to network. Everyone promises to get back to you. Just let me check a few things, and I WILL get back to you."

I'm still waiting.

\*

"We really must get together sometime."

More bullshit! We live less than five miles apart. There's a reason we haven't visited for fourteen years. If either of us had any intention of following through, we'd pick a date or at least offer to exchange numbers or e-mail addresses and say when we might call or write. Maybe we'll just "get back" to each other.

*

"How are you?" or "How you doin'?"

Although the questions seem harmless enough, the truth is, most people really don't care how you are. It's kind of like, "Hey, s'up?" How can you tell? The askers are either onto another subject or out of range before you have a chance to answer.

Sometimes "How are you?" is milked and churned until it's homogenized into something like "How are you feeling today?" or "How's everything going for you on this beautiful...?" But the greeter still doesn't care. A quick, dismissive response before the questioner has forgotten the question terminates the hollow exchange. If you really want to inquire about someone's health or well-being, at least wait for a reply.

I've actually seen a perky little Barbie sporting a wide distracted smile ask an apparent stranger in a wheelchair, hooked up to an oxygen tank and in obvious discomfort, "And how are you today?" Fortunately, Miss Smiley Face was out of range before the elderly gentleman articulated his most ungentlemanly response.

Depending on my mood, I will occasionally answer a blatantly rhetorical question with unanticipated compliance. It's a good way to unnerve a waiter, greeter, or just about anyone who doesn't know you and certainly hasn't been contemplating your health, but insists on asking anyway.

My conversation with a waiter:

"How are we doing today?"

*We?* "I just had a GI series and I'm hoping to get the results tomorrow, but it doesn't look good."

"Uh. Do you need more time?"

"Yeah. My bowels are a mess."

"I'll give you a few more minutes."

As the waiter slithered back towards the comfort of the restaurant's kitchen, I called, "Don't you want to hear about my brother's inflamed gall bladder?" *I guess not.*

*

Radio host Steve Somers has said, "Eighty percent of the people who ask about your problems don't care and the other twenty percent are glad you have them."

Makes sense to me.

## Are You F___n' Kidding Me?

The "F-bomb" has been around forever. (Do you ever wonder why no one has quoted General Custer's last words?) I don't claim innocence, though I only use it when the situation clearly calls for a bomb: "You're a f___n' idiot!"

Point is, you'd think this demonstrative, if questionable, term should accompany a loss of temper or at least suggest some degree of exasperation.

But now, among our latest generations, the bomb has steadily worked its way into everyday conversation. Whether it's peer pressure, the need to feel like a tough guy (or girl) or just another sign of a relaxed brain, the F-bomb has emerged as a major player in virtually every part of speech.

Some examples:

Adjective – "So I go to the f___n' store..."

Verb – "I told him not to f____ with me."

Noun – "I don't give a f____."

Adverb (as adjective modifier) – "That shirt's f____n' ugly."

Adverb (as verb modifier) – "So he's f____n' telling me..."

And, of course, your basic exclamatory – "Aw, f____!"

I can see how the F-bomb, though overused, can, at times, be worked into a discussion among friends. I can understand – sort of – how you can be so f____n' tired, or how something is so f____n' ridiculous, or how someone is so f____n' old, but how the f____ can you explain f____n' walking down the street? It seems a bit too casual for a bomb, doesn't it? I mean you can have to make that f____n' phone call, but how can you be f____n' making a phone call?

I was privy to another casual F-bomb recently as two young conversationalists passed me leaving the gym. One explained: "I'm gonna go back to f____n' jogging." Now I'm not familiar with this particular sport, but I imagine it would require remarkable flexibility, coordination, and endurance. Perhaps we'll see it in the Olympics someday, kind of a new twist on the Biathlon.

Sometimes the speaker is so intent on dropping an F-bomb that he'll use it before he knows what he wants to say. Recently overheard in the gym locker room: A young linguist who had already used the bomb in every conceivable grammatical context, as well as some inconceivable ones, said, "It's just f____n'..."

That was it! He was done talking! Now he was waiting for the other guy to pick up the "conversation." He'd used an F-bomb to introduce a thought he hadn't had yet!

## Translation, Please!

A few years ago, I heard two young "adults" calling to each other from across the street:

"Hey, chaet?"

"No, chew?"

"C'mon, lezgweet!"

Huh? As I walked about five city blocks, I replayed the cryptic exchange in my mind. When I finally decoded the "conversation," I realized the pair was planning a luncheon date:

"Hey. Did you eat?"

"No. Did you?"

"Come on. Let's go eat."

Why should it take a five-city-block walk to decipher your mother tongue?

## Euphemisms: A Kinder, Gentler Way of Misrepresenting Ourselves

The fast track to convoluted conversation is often paved with euphemisms – mild or vague expressions substituted for those that seem too harsh or offensive. Euphemisms are close relatives of language we call "politically correct."

Sometimes euphemisms are nothing more than harmless niceties. When advertisers once preferred inoffensive language like "skin blemishes," "dentures," "underarm wetness," and "irregularity" to uncomfortable words like "pimples," "false teeth," "sweat," and "constipation," they weren't trying to fool anyone. They communicated ideas, spared needless embarrassment, and perhaps made people feel better about themselves. No harm, no foul.

Similarly, telling someone a relative has "passed away" is kinder than the harsh truth that he'd "dropped dead." Saying, "Jerry can't come out to play because he's 'under the weather'" beats "Jerry is barfing all over his room." Again, no harm...

However, euphemisms become serious linguistic camouflage when they intentionally distort or misrepresent ideas. Some examples:

* People don't get fired; they are "released," which implies they've been granted the freedom to pursue other options.

* When a company decides to "downsize," it cleverly avoids the human element – that people have lost their jobs.

* "The subcommittee discovered many inaccuracies in the senator's statements" means "Senator Krum lied like a rug."

* "A renewed telecast" offers greater expectation than a mere "rerun."

* When the Bureau of Internal Revenue became the Internal Revenue Service in 1952, the implication was it was no longer a bureaucracy, but a service ready to serve you by collecting your taxes.

* See that ad for a "cozy home in a secluded area, free from the intrusions of daily life"? Congratulations! You've found an abandoned shack in the woods.

* I've heard a mother tell her eight-year-old son who was squashing produce in the supermarket that his behavior was "inappropriate." Glad you found a kind word, lady. I'm sure the pint-sized comparison shopper-in-training learned his lesson today.

* And let's not forget: "His spokesperson offered 'alternative facts' to refute the charges." (This one speaks for itself.)

## A linguistic see-through blouse

Sometimes euphemisms are intentionally transparent to create a dramatic effect while downplaying the severity of the message. Transparent euphemisms have always been a mainstay of mobster talk, as seen on TV and in the movies, with the language cleverly distorted to disguise criminal intent.

When the Godfather made someone an offer he "couldn't refuse," it sounded like a great deal, worthy of serious consideration. Of course, a reluctant customer risked waking in a bed with his favorite horse's head resting at his feet.

"We hope you will decide to sell your home so you can enjoy a long, happy life with your lovely wife and children" is clearly less offensive than the mobster's obvious (though unspoken) threat to kill the man and/or his family if he didn't agree to the sale.

\*

Many years ago, my wife and I experienced a blatantly transparent euphemism at a Rangers hockey game in New York's Madison Square Garden. As we took our places in the "blue seats" we soon realized how this notorious section got its well-deserved reputation. We were subjected to a constant barrage of unnervingly explicit rants (expletives not deleted) and howls – a virtual verbal manual on how hard to hit, where to hit, which bones to break, and which organs to render useless.

In the midst of the incessant vulgarities, we heard a most unanticipated euphemism as this huge "fan" hollered in a voice that dwarfed the blood-curdling masses: "Harass him! Harass him! Make him relinquish the puck!"

I guess that's what his friends were saying without resorting to euphemisms.

**No offense intended - or - "Your daughter finds things before people lose them."**

During my tenure as an inner-city teacher, I witnessed a growing affinity for euphemisms in order not to offend the parent, even if the little offender's behavior was strikingly offensive. Teachers were actually given written instructions defining appropriate and inappropriate language for parent-teacher conferences.

Here are a few examples:

| Don't Say: | Do Say: |
|---|---|
| Your child is rude. | Your child uses inappropriate language. |
| José is unpopular. | José needs to improve his socialization. |
| Lucretia steals from her classmates. | Lucretia must learn to share/doesn't always return… |
| Tanya talks too much. | Tanya must try harder to be quiet in class. |
| Michael copies Yolanda's homework. | Michael needs to put more personal effort into his homework. |

To me, this was just another attempt to hide behind euphemisms to soften and disguise the truth. I didn't believe in being rude, but to pacify a parent by making things seem better than they were simply wasn't an option for me. A bully is a bully is a bully – not someone who "exhibits aggressive behavior among his diminutive peers." A thief is a thief is a thief – not someone who "confuses ownership." Sometimes the truth hurts, but so do vapid, gratuitous platitudes.

Just for fun (and because this is my book), I've created my version of parent-teacher euphemisms. While I'm not suggesting we use this as a springboard to real conversation, I submit the following to illustrate, and, OK, ridicule our incessant groping for the politically correct comment:

| What They Wanted Us to Say: | What We Really Wanted to Say: |
|---|---|
| Henry must learn to control his body functions. | Henry burps and farts during silent reading. |
| George's social interactions are not what we had hoped for. | All the kids hate George. |
| Maria is quite mature for her age. | Maria is the only girl in second grade with multiple pierced body parts, eye shadow, and dates. |
| Tyrone needs to improve his personal hygiene. | Tyrone smells like he's carrying a dead animal in his shorts. |
| We find Damon's excuses to be somewhat disingenuous. | Damon is full of shit. |
| Juan talks excessively despite repeated warnings. | It's impossible to get your little bastard to shut up. |
| Marvin is intellectually challenged. | Marvin is dumb as a rock. |
| Buster is sexually inquisitive. | In the past three months, Buster has humped nearly half the freshman class. |

Again, I'm not advocating blatant rudeness. And while I realize uncensored and complete disclosure has its pitfalls, some parents do need an honest, constructive kick in the pants. In short, somewhere between the euphemism and the insult lies a truth waiting to be told.

## Listen, My Children...

Verbal communication is only possible if someone is actually listening. And if we've become a society of lazy and evasive talkers, we've simultaneously devolved into one that has conveniently forgotten the fine art of listening.

But in our never-ending effort to cover our disinterested asses, we've devised go-to expressions to give the impression we actually care what someone is saying:

Nowadays, people who "couldn't care less" (or is it "could care less"?) "hear you," "feel you," "know where you're coming from," and "feel your pain." How convenient to reach into a bag of stock answers and pull out a "hear you"/"feel you" response to any tale of woe about which we could/couldn't care less. It's nothing more than conversational clip art.

I have no doubt that if I told certain "listeners" (especially those in the 18-22 age group) I'm scheduled to have reconstructive surgery on both legs and an eye socket removed, they will have "been there; done that," or at the very least, they will "hear me," "feel me," and "know where I'm coming from." At times, these stock phrases can be genuine, if uninspired, responses. But more often than not, they're functions of conversational earwax.

Unfortunately, even the sincere listener will occasionally drop the ball. I remember one night shortly after my wife and I moved to our first apartment in Flushing, New York. We stepped into the elevator and were greeted by a sad-eyed, somewhat scruffy-looking little man who had apparently gotten on at the basement level. We returned his greeting and my wife, noticing his sorry state, offered a sincere and sympathetic, "How are you?"

His response was only slightly more intelligible than the lyrics of a Michael McDonald song. I replied, "I'm sorry" and my wife, almost simultaneously, said, "How nice. I'm glad for you."

When the stranger got off, I asked, "Why did you say you were glad his hair caught fire?"

"Fire? I thought he said he was here to retire."

Perhaps we would have been better off if we had just heard what he said - or knew where he was coming from. (I'm pretty sure it was the basement.)

# TELEPHONE TAG

"TELEPHONE, n. An invention of the devil which abrogates
some of the advantages of making a disagreeable person
keep his distance."
– Ambrose Bierce

**Thank you, Alexander Graham Bell!** Why didn't any of our inventive minds think of it sooner? Such a simple, yet profoundly game-changing, idea: Just pick up the telephone and, voila! – You're connected. Look how you've brought people together, without them having to get off the collective seats of their pants.

Mr. B, you'd be amazed to see how wildly popular your idea has become in the years following your historic first phone conversation in 1876: "Watson, get your ass in here! And why did I get a busy signal? Who the hell could you possibly have been talking to?"

## "Mother" of (an) Invention

Your invention has changed the very nature of our civilization, Alex. But were we satisfied with that? Evidently not. Over the years, we've actually "improved" the thing. Now I can make or receive a call from virtually anywhere, but even that's not enough for us anymore.

Modern technology has empowered us with "call waiting." Nowadays we get to choose who we want to call us. Instead of subjecting me to the "indignity" of a busy signal, the callee may elect to put me on hold while he exhausts an existing conversation. When we are at last verbally engaged, he can decide to interrupt our chat or terminate it altogether, depending on the value he places on an incoming call.

At times, I may find myself on speakerphone. This allows the person at the other end of the line to go about his business and talk to me without holding the phone (we call this "multitasking"), while my voice resounds throughout his room. Unfortunately, this produces an echo chamber and/or staticky effect, making it hard for us to understand each other, except for the inevitably too late warning that I should watch what I'm saying because so-and-so can hear me. I almost always manage to offend someone I had no idea was in the room.

## Giving Us the Business

Alexander, your ingenious invention really gets interesting when I make a business call. Corporate America has taken your brilliant idea to levels of agony and frustration you never could have envisioned.

When I call a company or an organization, the first thing I hear is, "Listen carefully because our menu has changed." I never knew so many businesses that weren't restaurants had menus. But now each company has a menu. And its menu has "changed." So I "listen carefully." After an interminable array of choices, I hear my other options: "If you have a rotary phone, please visit our website at www.wescrewyou.com or e-mail us at ripoff.org." If I still own a rotary phone, what are the chances I have the technology to visit your damn website?

## Holding Tactics

After listening carefully and selecting one of four hundred

options, I am immediately placed on hold and informed, "All agents are busy assisting other customers." Unfortunately, the company is experiencing "unusually high call volume" – as usual. But I'm assured I will speak to the "next available agent."

Now I'm on hold for the one agent who has opted to show up for work that day. Apparently the firm believes I need to be entertained while I maintain my holding pattern. So how about some music? Here's a delightful little tune from hell called, "I Wouldn't Take Her to a Dawg Fight, 'Cause I'm Afraid She'd Win."

Whatever song the company has chosen to delight me with as I endure the interminable hold only adds to my growing urge to strangle someone. The "music" is loud enough to invite friends over and party.

Often while the company's got me on hold, it will use the opportunity to shamelessly promote all its products and services. After describing itself as a blend of the Red Cross, UNICEF, Mother Teresa, and the Apostles and exhausting every last ounce of gratuitous self-praise and useless information, it may finally connect me to an agent who was perhaps not so busy.

This eventual human voice might belong to Molly in Sales, who talks to me just long enough to conclude I've got the wrong extension. *Wasn't I supposed to push number 74?*

"You want to speak to Carrie in Customer Service. Please hold."

After a few more stanzas: "Hello. Customer Service."

"Is this Carrie?"

"Yes. Please hold."

More music, then another voice: "Hello, this is Linda. Can I help you?"

"I was holding for Carrie."

"What do you need?"

I give Linda all the details.

"I can help you, sir. Please hold."

So now I'm holding for Carrie, Linda, or perhaps Molly.

Then there's this uneasy silence and I'm actually hoping the "music" will return. "Hello? Hello?" *Oh shit!*

No one answers. A damn dial tone! Carrie, Linda, and perhaps Molly have all disappeared into the telephone's "Black Hole" and I'm left helplessly clutching my disconnected instrument of communication.

## Staying Disconnected

Before forgetting about me, a company will repeatedly play this reminder: "Your call is very important to us. Please continue to hold." At some point, I can expect to hear that eerie silence followed by a dial tone or those fateful words: "If you'd like to make a call, please hang up and dial again." Either way, my "very important call" has been disconnected.

*

Here's my favorite disconnect story: When my daughter moved out years ago, we no longer needed her separate landline so I called the phone company to have it disconnected. After a lengthy round of irrelevant questioning and exasperating explanations ("No, I don't want to terminate all phone service..."), I was told to speak to the Disconnect Department. The representative transferred me and, after a brief moment of silence, I heard, "If you want to make a call..." They disconnected me!

I called back and, with a surprising display of civility, explained the irony – "I was disconnected by Disconnect! I didn't want my call disconnected, you technological whiz. I wanted..." Eventually, I was reconnected to Disconnect, who finally lived up to their name and disconnected the one line I no longer needed.

## At Your (Cable) Service

A call to my cable company to report a loss of Internet service (yet again) elicited nearly every known telephone-answering/stalling technique, none of which included putting a technician on the line to address my problem.

I pressed "1" for English, listened to the "revised" menu (which hadn't changed in eleven years), and then, as I had so many times before, pressed "4" for Internet Repair. I was advised that all agents were busy aggravating other customers, but my call was very important and would be answered by the next available agent. Meanwhile, I was forced to endure a detailed catalog of the many services available to the company's "highly valued" customers and was then entertained by some gut-wrenching music.

After several rounds of mindless propaganda and song, I put the phone down and attended to some long-neglected chores. Since I don't have speakerphone service, I placed the phone near my work area so I'd be available should the promos and music be replaced by a live human voice during my remaining coherent years.

Not only was the wait long enough for me to reorganize most of my workroom, by the time I heard the distant shouts of, "Hello! Hello!" I'd forgotten that I made a call and wondered why there was a phone on the freezer next to my workbench. However, after a few leading questions from the technician, I remembered the problem.

Before continuing, my technical advisor said he needed to confirm my address. I explained that since I had dialed for service, we'd moved to a new neighborhood and the kids were now grown...Nothing. Not a clue. The "joke" was lost on him. Maybe I should have pressed number 2, for Spanish. *¿Quien* *sabe?*

## It's Sam, I Am

Sometimes, after an immediate connection, you may still not be quite as "connected" as you'd hoped. For computer problems that are not cable-related, you must call the manufacturer who will immediately put you in touch with "Rick" or "Phil" or "Todd" who are outsourced halfway around the world in Pakistan, India, the Philippines, Malaysia, or some Third World country where it would be safe to say they've never even met a Rick or Phil or Todd. But computer companies believe their American customers are more comfortable talking to Todd than to Achmed.

So when my computer failed me, I made the call. My assigned computer maven du jour, "Sam," valiantly struggled with the English language while he tried to display a sense of unjustified confidence in his technical skills. This did not bode well for fixing my computer since I need to be led like a child through *Computers for Dummies*. I don't expect everyone to be proficient in my native tongue, but it was Sam's job to communicate instructions in a specific language – and I had pressed "1" for English.

Our verbal exchange went something like this:

"Hello. This is Sam. What am I doing to you today?"

"I was hoping you could help fix my computer." I identified myself and explained the problem.

"This is no problem, Mr. Larry. Please turn off computer." (Pause) "What do you see?"

"Nothing. The computer is off."

"This is good. Turn on computer."

I spent the next hour pressing keys in every fathomable combination and although to Sam everything was "good," I noticed nothing was being fixed. I'm sure if I'd told him the computer had exploded and my house was on fire, he would have said, "This is good."

Then Sam decided on a new approach. He had me unplug and re-plug wires from the computer and the modem into different sockets throughout the house. "Pull wire, hold wire, swallow wire... "

"What? Oh, 'follow wire.'"

"Plug it in; pull it out..."

Then, out of nowhere: "How is the weather, Mr. Larry?"

*What the hell?* "It's raining."

"Is hot here."

"I don't care."

After two hours of incredible futility, not only was I hopelessly tangled in computer wire, the computer was working less efficiently than before, my TV was flickering, and my wife was complaining that other household devices were failing. I demanded that Sam return my computer to the way it was when I could at least turn on my kitchen lights. After countless rounds of plugging and unplugging, hitting keys and occasionally the wall, my computer was "restored" to its original compromised condition. "That's it!" I screamed.

"The TV's working and so is the toaster!" my wife yelled.

Then Sam asked a question that will remain forever engraved in my mind. "Is there anything else I can do to help you with today?"

I "politely" suggested he could immediately hang up and help someone else.

This led to a final "Thank you, Mr. Larry. I am in pleasure to be..."

Click.

## Does Medi Care?

Medicare is a wonderful resource for those of us who've

celebrated enough birthdays to qualify for this bastion of essential services – unless you actually need to speak to someone. After my first telephone experience with my new health provider, I have made every effort to avoid verbal contact with this bane of my "Golden Years." But sometimes there's no avoiding it.

Occasionally, Medicare declines payment for medical services because, for reasons no one can explain, it has reverted to my secondary provider's ID number and will only rectify the error through direct contact with the innocent victim of its negligence. (That would be me.) Since failure to remunerate unnerves a doctor more than a malignant tumor, I must close my eyes, grit my teeth, take the plunge, and dial.

When calling Medicare, it doesn't take long to realize you have not dialed Planet Fitness. "Thank you for calling Medicare. To continue in English..."

*Blah, blah.*

"Have your Medicare card ready. Be prepared to provide your Medicare number or to have someone read it for you. If you don't have your card with you, take a moment to look for it. If you are unable to find your card, have someone help you find it. Have them lift you up if it is too high, help you down if it's too low...

"Make sure you have any necessary papers ready or have someone..." (I have everything laid out from my birth certificate to my latest rejection of payment.) "Our agents are busy tormenting other subscribers. The approximate waiting time is twelve years."

Eventually, I hear: "Medicare. Mrs. Kranz speaking."

"Hello," I say. "This is Larry Berliner. I realize you were waiting for me to pass away, but I'm glad I finally..."

"State your full name and address."

No chuckle at the other end. No hint of a sense of humor.

*Are you related to the cable guy?* I dutifully recite my full name and address.

"Your card number, your date of birth, your father's mother's maiden name, the date your middle child began eating solid food..."

Done, done, done – and though I have no middle child – done.

"What is your problem, sir?"

"The problem is you have the wrong ID for me."

"Oh, you need to speak to the Quasi-Cerebral Undermining Unit at 555-8431."

"Please connect me."

"You must dial the number directly."

So, with a broken spirit, and aging like a mayfly, I dial the new number.

"Thank you for calling Medicare. To continue in English..."

*

Thanks anyway, Mr. Bell. It seemed like a good idea at the time.

# CELL PRIVILEGES

"You speak an infinite deal of nothing."
– William Shakespeare

**Let me make one thing** perfectly clear: Despite what people say, I am not a cell phone hater. I love my cell phone; I only hate yours. That's because *I* control my cell phone. It's a convenient little modern device that serves a purpose when immediate contact is necessary.

The operative word here is "necessary." If I'm stuck in traffic, I can call ahead and inform an interested party that I'm going to be late. The receiver of my call can sit tight and wait or we can revise our plans. If the once interested party has lost interest and prefers that I simply turn around, he or she can say so and spare me the rest of the trip.

Why do I hate *your* cell phone? Because you constantly abuse its primary purpose and often infringe on my privacy, interrupt my agenda, even compromise my safety in your relentless, often ill-advised, quest to stay connected.

## On the Boardwalk

My first experience with your cell phone was in the early 1990s on the boardwalk in Ocean City, Maryland. My wife and I had just gotten seated on a tram when a slovenly 20-

something guy sitting in front of us and yakking away on his cell phone, turned around and asked us to "keep it down." I informed the rude conversationalist that he was not in a phone booth and encouraged him to find one. Little did I know that this talkative smartass was ahead of his time and that, in the years to follow, I would be subjected to intrusive phone conversations in virtually every public venue.

## In the Post Office

Waiting my turn on line, I heard this conversation:
Clerk: "Would you like delivery confirmation?"
Customer on phone: "So she says to me, 'Mama, I need...' What? One minute. Yes, delivery confirmation. What? No, she didn't have the baby..."
*C'mon, lady! I just want to mail a letter and buy a book of stamps.*

## In the Supermarket

Here you will invariably find a frazzled husband on the phone, frantically trying to clarify his mission. "Honey, where are the little ice cream bars with the vanilla centers? They don't have the big rolls of toilet paper on sale, so should I get...?"

This scene is actually more amusing than intrusive. We've all been there – desperately struggling to get it right. But how did well-intentioned husbands navigate the supermarket before cell phones? We reviewed our options, made our own decisions, went home, and took our comeuppance like men.

### Breakup in aisle 6!

Not all supermarket intrusions are amusing or easily overlooked. One day, my wife was shopping for produce when she heard a man's voice in the next aisle, among the assorted berries and green peppers, in a one-sided "conversation" bellowing at his apparent girlfriend, with whom he was apparently breaking up. Unfortunately, no one intervened to advise this fool that he was distracting and annoying other customers – in addition to wilting the lettuce.

Surely the object of his disaffection was in another public place answering his de-mating call. Wouldn't it be cool if a female customer had the nerve to yell into his phone: "Hey, handsome, my motor's running!"?

## In a Restaurant

This is another preferred, but inappropriate place for a clearly irrelevant, non-essential, often needlessly loud, cell phone conversation.

At a popular resort, my wife and I were seated in an open booth in a small cafe opposite four people, apparently two couples, and all four were chatting on cell phones! We wondered why none of them was with the person he/she was talking to.

Why do people never seem to be with the folks they want to talk to? Here's a novel idea: Hang out with people you enjoy chatting with. Then you won't have to call them when you're socializing with others.

## In the Gym

Of all places where a cell phone would seem to be an unnecessary device, a gym or health club would head my list. To me, a gym is where you go to get away from life's problems and annoyances, including its intrusive technology. Unless you're awaiting an important medical result or some other urgent call, why can't you leave the damn phone in the locker room with your jacket and long pants?

I've seen these faux health enthusiasts on the phone during virtually every physical activity:

* On the treadmill: "Hey, wazzup? No, this is cool. I'm on the treadmill. Let me speed this mother up a few notches. Yeah, now I'm movin' – Oh, shit!"
* On the exercise mat: "Wazzup? 21, 22, 23...No, we cool. You got 10? 11, 12, 13...What time tonight? 8? 9, 10, 11..."
* Lifting weights: "F____n' heavy. Ahhhhh!"
* On the machines: "Yeah, it's the abdominal exercise something. What? Your mother needs abdominal..."

I guess I'm the one who doesn't get it. I just go to the gym to work out.

*

I find it intriguing to observe the unraveling of a well-intentioned workout on the Roman Chair – an elevated apparatus with a back, two armrests, handgrips, and no seat. The exerciser lays both arms on the rests, grasps the hand grippers, and lifts his/her legs in a variety of ab-blasting poses – knees bent, legs straight, one leg at a time – and then repeats.

It's a simple and effective routine – unless you need to answer the phone. To do this, you must either bend your head impossibly to one side or lift an arm so it relinquishes contact with the classically designed armrest. This is where voluntary movement succumbs to the Law of Gravity. I've seen more than one cell phone addict who preferred cellular gratification to cellulite reduction, rudely exit the Roman Chair in mid-call and land unceremoniously on his or her gluteus maximus.

*

Most annoying is watching a gym member yakking into his cell phone while resting on a piece of equipment I was hoping to use. Can we assume these machines were designed to accommodate moving body parts other than flapping lips?

Someone tell these people that sitting on an incline bench or rowing machine for half an hour while talking on the phone does not count as exercise.

After waiting a reasonable time and concluding the babbling squatter has no intention of utilizing the bench press, pec deck, or seated curl machine any time during this calendar year, I respectfully ask, "Can I work in? I'd like to sit here and make a call."

The wannabe gym rat will proudly announce he's worked out for two hours. News flash: Not counting changing, washing, shaving, casual bullshitting and unlimited cell phone service, you worked out for seven minutes. Go home, you lazy, misguided clown! You might as well have stayed in bed.

## In the Locker Room

There's always a lot of chatter in the locker room of my health club. Unfortunately, about fifty percent of this banter involves people who aren't present. Can't you take your cell phone to a corner of the room, or out of the room – or into heavy traffic? But who am I to spurn a twenty-first century tradition?

It's even more disturbing when I'm the only one in the locker room. Someone enters with a big, "Hey, how are you?"

"I'm good," I answer.

Then I hear the one-way conversation continue: "Cool! When did you get back?"

"Excuse me? I was the only one in the room so I..." Oh, forget it. BTW, you're allowed to succumb to this ruse only once. (Maybe twice – if it's hands free.)

## In the Toilet Stall

You never know when you'll stumble upon an improbable situation during routine activities.

One day, after doing some quick "business" and washing my hands before hitting the gym, I heard a voice from the only closed bathroom stall. This presented two unpleasant possibilities:

He had a friend in there. (Quickly eliminated – One set of feet and only one voice talking.)

That left possibility number two: He was on the damn cell phone!

Really? This brought a whole new disgusting dimension to multi-tasking. It soon became obvious that this loquacious squatter had initiated the conversation. (OK, I lingered a while.) Why now, fool? Has the cell phone become a twenty-first century laxative?

Hearing a serious business discussion randomly interrupted by farts and splashes bordered on an out-of-body experience. (Poor choice of words?)

Then from nowhere: "Shit!" (An emphatic reaction or a plaintive cry for relief?) "My stuff is in the toilet." (OK. He didn't really say that.)

Here's a scary thought: I hope he remembered which hand was holding the phone when he finished his other business and had to wrap up the ill-timed conversation. Didn't he have to re-grab the cell phone before exiting the stall? There were too many revolting possibilities. I know it wasn't hands-free because he'd already dropped the damn thing. (Ugh!)

**I am not alone**

Not long ago, my wife found this posted by a woman on Facebook:

OMG!...I was in the public restroom – I was barely sitting down when I heard a voice in the other stall: "Hi, how are you?"

Me: (embarrassed) "Doin' fine!"

Stall: "So what are you up to?"

Me: "Uhhh, I'm like you, just sitting here."

Stall: "Can I come over?"

Me: (attitude) "No, I'm a little busy right now!"

Stall: "Listen, I'll have to call you back. There's an idiot in the other stall who keeps answering all my questions!"

## In the Car

I'm tired of having my ride threatened by chatty motorists who refuse to wait until they stop the car to whip out the phone.

Fortunately, this distraction has been "solved" with the hands-free Bluetooth device. Now the driver, driven to pursue that all-consuming, if irrelevant, cell phone conversation, can keep both hands on the wheel. Unfortunately, his/her (mostly her) brain, as free as her hands, is still focused on a flippant cell phone conversation, rather than the multi-ton vehicles driven by other distracted navigators of the open road.

I've seen motorists use their hands-free opportunities to read road maps! Why the hell are you reading a map? You're never going to get there!

### Relatively speaking

I have a close relative (not to be identified here out of respect for my only daughter), who is convinced the best time to call is when she's driving. "What else is there to do, Dad?"

"Uh, drive?"

The conversation generally goes like this: "Yak, yak, blah, blah...Where the hell am I?"

Once she actually had an accident while we were talking on the phone. She quickly reassured me she was OK, knowing that was my main concern. (I'd wait until later to discuss my other issues.)

As a worried father, my inclination has always been to get her off the phone, but since I know I'll be immediately replaced by another yakker, I stay on, hoping I can at least steer the conversation - if not the car.

## In Line for a Vacation

As we stood on the hotel's check-in line, I glanced around the crowded lobby and spotted two, maybe three of the dozens of would-be vacationers who were not on their cell phones. Some actually passed up their turns at the check-in counter, so intent were they on consummating their crucial conversations. Give it a rest! You left those people behind for a reason.

## Viva Las Vegas!

Cell phones have apparently spawned a society of rocket scientists and brain surgeons who need to chronicle their every move. This compulsion to remain connected became most evident to me a few years ago when my wife and I spent a week in Las Vegas.

Remember, this was Las Vegas. If you can't find something to grab your attention there, you might as well vacation in New Jersey. Yet wherever we went – wherever cell phones were permitted (and a few places where they weren't) – phones were turned on and vacationers were tuned in to the songs of these hand-held Sirens.

I recall one evening walking from the Tropicana to the nearby MGM Grand amidst a relentless mass of single-minded humanity, fervently clutching their precious communication devices. You'd think we were all part of a documentary on walking the celebrated streets of Las Vegas. There was nary a person with two free ears, making it virtually impossible to avoid being privy to someone's inane conversation. If we walked faster, we just entered the airspace of another self-indulgent chronicler. It didn't matter whose signal we picked up; they were all the same:

"I'm going to see Stout Snout and the Nasal Hairs. Now I'm waiting for the light to change. OK, it's green. I'm crossing the street. Damn crowded. I crossed the street. Excuse me – some people..." (Author's note: both on phone) "I'm approaching the theater. Ouch! You %#*^!" (Yet again) "I'm going into the theater. Showing my ticket." (Pause) "Shit! Dropped the damn phone. I'm not cursing, ma'am. Yes, I'm turning it off."

Thankfully, cell phones must be deactivated (at least theoretically) during most headline performances. Unfortunately, this often-abused mandate expires with the end of the show. As we left the theater, the cell phones reappeared en masse. "I saw the show...I'm leaving the building...I'm crossing the street."

Who the hell are these people? Who cares? Who needs to know when they cross the damn street? My wife and I enjoyed the show and afterwards we talked about it. Wasn't anyone in the company of someone they wanted to talk to?

If we wanted to share this experience with relatives and friends, we'd call them later – or better still – we'd send postcards.

In my fantasy, the cell phone junkie recites: "We're crossing Las Vegas Boulevard...The light is changing...Have to hurry...Tourist bus coming...All Star Tours...Got all the hotels on its side...What a skyline...Hey, it's...Oh, sh..."

Then, five minutes later – "I'm in an ambulance, going to the emergency room...Yes, I'll call when we get there. Owww!"

## Thank You, Doctor. May I Have Another?

I realize some people need to be accessible 24/7: doctors, emergency/security/law enforcement personnel, pubescent teens... During my tenure as an inner-city English teacher, I never felt the need to subject myself to indiscriminate access.

Even my landline number was unlisted. What was the likelihood of an urgent call demanding instant clarification on how to use a metaphor or where to place that troublesome apostrophe?

I know essential service people see things from their unique perspectives. For example, I'm sure my urologist has been called in without notice for emergency...urology stuff and has learned to depend on his cell phone as a vital extension of his practice.

This would explain his reaction to my phone being off during my annual digital rectal exam. (This is where the doctor sticks his finger up your ass – approximately to his elbow – to determine the size of your prostate.) During the procedure, he likes to revert to small talk, presumably to take your mind off your discomfort. When I mentioned I had turned off my cell phone, he asked, "Why would you do that?"

"Doctor," I squeezed out through gritted teeth, "do you think – Ouch! – I want to get a call now?"

*

Never mind electricity and indoor plumbing. How did we ever exist without cell phones? How did we drive our cars, cross the street, walk the dog, wait to be served in a restaurant, stand on line, sit in a doctor's waiting room?

And so, as I continue to navigate through a world of phone zombies who can't bear to separate themselves from their technological appendages, I'll just keep my cell phone set to "off" until I decide to use it.

## And the Cell Phone Begat...

No discussion of the cell phone would be complete without mentioning its bastard offspring – one that should have been aborted at conception – the all-too-popular phone text messaging. Like its verbally abused parent, phone texting has its time and place, though, in my opinion, its use should be limited to, "Help!"

Now that we've explored its positive feature, I submit a few negatives:

\* Texting Creates an Avoidable Safety Hazard

I've yet to grasp the need to "stay connected" while operating a motor vehicle. As if the cell phone doesn't provide ample opportunity for self-annihilation, phone texting further lowers the sanity bar. Yet some who walk – and drive – among us have no problem texting while driving. Where better to keep in touch than on the Interstate at 70-miles-per-hour?

Would you carry an old-fashioned portable typewriter on your lap while driving? Would you work on your laptop or iPad or read a business report behind the wheel of a car? (You, maybe.) How is phone texting any safer? How many people have begun their final text message: "Oh, what a beautiful..."?

\* Texting Paves the Road to Illiteracy

If, as some suggest, writing is a lost art, phone-texting has finally put it to rest under a mound of tightly packed dirt. Texting encourages lazy writing with intentional misspellings, incomplete sentences, omitted punctuation, and an endless series of ridiculous emoticons and ever-changing abbreviations, all in the interest of speed.

The seasoned texter leaves out all "unnecessary" letters, especially vowels, and even replaces a few sounds with numbers: CRDTCHCK (Credit check), CUL8R (See you later), FTBOMH (From the bottom of my heart), 2G2BT (Too good to be true), HHOK (Ha ha, only kidding), or, better still: HHO1/2K (Ha, ha – only half kidding).

Have we created a new language or are we simply, and I do mean "simply," dumbing down? After all, a child's first attempts at language generally consist of pronouncing the first letter sound of each word and dropping vowels in a primal attempt to communicate.

Sure, we've all used some common abbreviations to enliven and vary communication: (RSVP, ASAP, FYI, TGIF). But for some people, abbreviated English has become the language of choice and this trendy mutant consumes nearly the whole damn message. Eventually the only sentence a youngster will understand is the one Uncle Ralph is serving in the Big House. BTW, if the recipient has to devote precious minutes trying to decipher an unfamiliar abbreviation, doesn't that waste the time you're trying to save? Gotta keep the line moving.

Someone tell me why "prolly" is preferred to "probably." How much time did you save by dropping three letters, adding one and prolly...er...probably forgetting how to spell a real word in the prcs?

\*

If you can't beat 'em...Why not give us seniors a place in this BNW of yours? As seen on the Internet:

SENIOR CITIZEN TEXTING CODES
ATD – At the Doctor
BFF – Best Friend Fell
BYOT – Bring Your Own Teeth
FWIW – Forgot Where I Was
LMDO – Laughing My Dentures Out
ROFLACGU – Rolling on Floor Laughing and Can't Get Up

\*

I realize I might be offending an entire generation, but frankly kids, IDC. Fact is, no matter how quickly and easily you write your message, this dumbed-down method of trendy, slipshod communication will eventually leave you AFU.

\* Texting Leads to Confusion and Misunderstandings

Even w/o those cursed abbreviations, hasty writing leads to mangled messaging. I've seen friendships and marriages strained to their limits by careless texting. Sometimes all it takes is hitting the wrong button: "Marvin's wife is really stupid and boring." This was sent, inadvertently, to Marvin's wife! Ouch! And what about the dreaded "Reply All" when you intended to reply to only one person? TFMDC (Time For More Damage Control).

\*

In the land of the texter, where context is ignored, ambiguity rules:

"Jenny likes sex more than her husband." (A satisfied customer or a promiscuous wench?)

"Linda's mom remarried when she was 7." (Ah, young love!)

\*

If you haven't got time for a vowel, a well-placed apostrophe is out of the question:

"My teacher called the students names."

\*

Think end punctuation doesn't matter?

"Thirteen people showed up for the party."

"Thirteen people showed up for the party?"

"Thirteen people showed up for the party!"

\*

Just in case we haven't relinquished enough of our working brains to technology, along comes auto-fill. If your cell phone has this dandy little feature, it will automatically complete your thoughts for you. Hard to imagine anything going wrong here.

You want to say, "Our first date was terrific." But instead you send, "Our first date was terrible." "You make me feel important" becomes "You make me feel impotent."

*

I heard this conversation at the mall:
"Why did you text me I look awful?"
"What! I said you look awesome."
"You wrote 'awful.'"
"I didn't mean...Cindy! Come back here!"

*

And finally, another Facebook post:
"Damn you, talk-to-text auto correct...if I don't enunciate then you spell it wrong so I speak orthopedic and you friggen send 'ortho P dick' and I hit send to my 14 yr old daughter."

## Summing up

Of course, all this off-track sweating could be avoided, or at least minimized, if the sender took the time to proofread, but the determined texter will have none of that. Kind of defeats the purpose, doesn't it? Time-consuming proofreading is incongruous with thoughtless speedwriting.

*

The bottom line is whether it's an ambiguous thought, careless punctuation, computerized sentence completion, or those endless, creative abbreviations, your precious texting sends the wrong message.

# LA VIDA LOCA

# AT YOUR SERVICE – NOT!

"Nowhere a woman so busy of her class,
And yet she seemed much busier than she was."
– Geoffrey Chaucer
(Adapted from *The Canterbury Tales*)

**Ah! Dining out.** A chance for the wife and me to forget the petty (and not-so-petty) demands of our daily lives or to at least relegate them for a few hours to the back burners of our minds. Dining out has always been a highly anticipated respite from the leaky roof, screaming children, inflamed prostate (that would be me), overdue bills – all the little distractions that make life interesting, way too interesting. It's our time, however brief, to unwind, relax, sit back, order, and consume.

## Yes, I Remember It Well

When I recall our dining out experiences, one particular evening at a local Greek family-owned diner always comes to mind. I can still see us entering the unpretentious eatery to the welcoming aromas of some serious grilling, roasting, and baking. Our seats overlook the parking lot, but we hardly notice the lack of ambiance as we hungrily peruse the food list and quickly make our dinner choices. Then we close our menus and scan the area expectantly. (We know a closed menu signals the waiter you are ready to order.)

## "Good Evening. I'm Your Worst Nightmare."

After the menus have been visibly closed and the room has been thoroughly scanned and virtually memorized, our apparent waitress bursts into the dining area like she's been slingshot from the kitchen, her head on a swivel as if auditioning for a Jack the Ripper flick. All the while, she's engaged in a heated conversation with – herself. Our longed-for ride on the sea of tranquility seems headed for choppy waters.

That someone resembling a waitress finally appears is not to suggest she actually stays to take our order or asks what we would like to drink or brings bread or, in fact, performs any waitress-related function. She simply touches my shoulder as she scoots past us (to acknowledge our existence or to signal me that she is lonely?) and comes to a screeching halt at a nearby table. There she is accosted by a starving couple who demand to know where she's been for the past fortnight.

Her answer is a breathless, "It's been a rough day, my darlings. What can I get you?"

After taking their order, the clearly overmatched waitress looks around trying to remember where she left us, then boldly steps up, pad and pencil in hand – her right hand, as I recall. Her left hand is used to steady herself on the back of my chair. "OK, my dears. What are we having tonight?"

She then proceeds to drop her pad and pencil onto my lap. The "lady" retrieves her pad with little difficulty, but takes three stabs at the pencil before lifting it from where it landed on my crotch. "That's not your pencil!" I announce at the second stab.

"Sorry, darling. OK, my dears," she repeats. "What are we having tonight?"

Indiscriminate "darlings" and "dears" have always left me a bit queasy, but when a waitress wants to know what "we" are having, two thoughts immediately occur to me: *I didn't know you were joining us* and *Uh oh, another kindergarten teacher.*

I voice neither thought since I know both will be lost on her and besides, I'm really hungry. No sense in consuming extra time, especially since I have this growing fear that perhaps time is all we'll be consuming.

## Do You Want Food With That?

We recite our orders, daring to hope that what we get will vaguely resemble what we've asked for as she continually looks over her shoulder and poses disturbing questions like, "Would you prefer your soup with your salad?"

After politely requesting a timely separation of courses, we dismiss our waitress, wondering if we will meet again anytime soon and whether dishes of food might then change hands.

My wife does utter one last plaintive cry: "Could we please have some bread and water?"

"I'll send the busboy," comes the distant call and I notice a bevy of heads rising in wishful anticipation.

## What's in a Word?

Eventually, a young man arrives carrying a towel, but unfortunately, nothing else. For some unfathomable reason, he then proceeds to clean our table. Not wanting to appear ungrateful for this attentive, though totally unnecessary service (we haven't yet had an opportunity to soil anything), I thank him for his well-intentioned, if ill-advised, efforts.

I emphatically repeat our growing need to assuage our appetites with bread and water. Then, as our Hispanic Felix Unger gives the pristine surface one last buff, he looks at me, beaming with a sense of pride one can only muster from cleaning an already spotless table and says, *"No hablo Ingles."*

Not to worry. Recalling my high school Spanish, I blurt out, "We need *pan y...*Shit!" *What the hell is the word for..."Agua!"* That's it! *Pan y agua!"*

Unfortunately, by the time I utter the correct word, Señor Unger has already headed for the kitchen. "Sweetheart," I whisper. "I think I just ordered bread and shit."

## Thar She Blows!

Our waitress again explodes on the scene, swiveling perhaps a bit less (perhaps not) and gingerly holding a bowl of soup.

"Who ordered soup?" our service-challenged server announces. A dozen hands shoot up.

"What kind is it?" asks a voice from the next table.

"Some kind of bean."

Our hearts sink as we distinctly remember ordering some kind of chowder. After finally connecting the dots for the soup, she is off again. "I didn't forget you, my darlings," she calls to us.

*Again with the "darlings."*

"Could we just have some bread and..."

"I've only got two hands," are the last words I hear as the waitress disappears into the kitchen where there is obviously some serious cooking going on. (We've noticed waiters proudly marching by with stacks of consumables on their trays.)

## Is this Table Taken?

On her next fly-by, having completed her appointed rounds – at least to her satisfaction – does our waitress check her customers to see if everything is OK? Not exactly. Apparently exhausted from effectively postponing a feeding frenzy, she squeezes herself into a nearby booth and strikes up a conversation with two couples who are harmlessly occupying themselves with bread and salad.

For some reason, this famished foursome does not summarily evict her. Instead they politely listen to her rant while munching on their reheated rolls and wilting greens.

Evidentally not content with being seated and marginally accepted, our imprudent server gesticulates wildly and knocks one man's glass of Merlot, Cabernet Sauvignon, or Shiraz from his hand. I'm sure it was a red wine because, while indiscernible in the glass, it reveals itself vividly on the tablecloth and on the the gentleman's white pants.

The waitress then hastily excuses herself, leaving the bewildered couples sitting in stunned disbelief, uncertain whether to eat, wipe, scream, or sue.

## Fed Up With Diogenes

The owner materializes – a short, balding, chubby man, walking with obvious uncertainty and holding a single glass of soda. He is the essence of Diogenes, a coke for his lantern, searching not (like his Greek proprototype) for an "honest man," but for a thirsty customer. He surveys the nutritionally-deprived assembly as he seeks to unite patron and beverage.

Seizing the opportunity, I ask our modern-day truth-seeker if he could seek out some bread and water.

"I'll get the busboy," he offers as he continues his relentless mission.

## Bus Stop

Our well-intentioned table buffer reappears with bread and – thank God! – water.

*"Muchas gracias,"* I say, trying not to sound like a linguistic novice struggling with *Hooked on Los Phonics* and ever so

grateful he did not act on my earlier bi-lingual request.

A few moments later (moments, minutes, years...), a second busboy makes the fateful walk down Starvation Alley with another supply of *pan y agua*. Desperate arms reach out like convicts groping from their prison cells and plaintive cries beg for sustenance. The overwhelmed server screams for mercy in some undetermined language, surrenders his offerings to the nearest table, and disappears, though not before overturning the one food-filled dish in our sector.

## Fed at Last

Our waitress finally emerges, uncomfortably carrying two soup bowls to our table while cursing her pain from the spillage onto her exposed fingers. Then, can it be? A busboy with our salads! At least I think they are our salads. The dressings are a bit questionable, but as my wife so eloquently proclaims: "Screw the dressing!"

The waitress from hell is off again and, shouting words that strike us like a Parthean shaft, calls: "I'll be right back with your entrées!"

With our mouths full of soup and salad, we try to articulate, "Not yet!"

"Let's finish our soup before it gets cold," my wife says. "We can have the salads for dessert."

Actually, I'd planned on having dessert for dessert.

Then Diogenes, having successfully dispensed his one glass of soda, returns holding a single plate of food. A young freedom fighter wearing a bandana and showing some ominous tattoos running the length of both arms, cradles another entrée.

"Those go to Table 26," calls the gray blur (now sporting a bandage on her damaged digits). Table 26, we notice, is putting on their coats and suggesting to Diogenes that his waitress place their long-overdue dinners in a most unappetizing setting.

Another Rambo clone ambles up to our table. "You finished with that soup?"

I look at the potatoes and vegetables lying innocently in the virtually untouched broth. "Not really... "

"I gotta make room for the other stuff," he says, removing our bread as a small brigade of guerrillas, each holding a single dish or two, surround the table.

I reclaim the bread. We clutch our soup. The salads seem safe; the table-top warriors don't appear interested in them.

"Just put it all there!" calls Mary f____n' Poppins, pointing to our table as she flies by, bringing her version of famine relief to the emaciated masses yearning to be fed.

## Exhuming the Remains

Before devouring our long-awaited dinners, we take on the roles of crime-scene investigators as we try to determine the species of our entrées before they were sliced, diced, roasted, or fried. After a hasty visual autopsy, I suggest, "This could be your duck. It has legs."

My wife surveys the dish. "Aren't these legs a little small? I mean the whole duck looks..."

"I think I got your duck." We look up as a tall, middle-aged woman approaches our table holding a dish of food. She then identifies the charred carcass of her Cornish hen resting in my wife's plate and we proceed to exchange entrées.

Our visitor then returns to her table where her husband holds his head while repeatedly stabbing the table with a steak knife. "I asked for a spoon," he mutters through gritted teeth. "Who the hell uses a steak knife for soup?"

"Since when does a rib roast have legs?" cries a voice from a nearby table.

At least we've all apparently been treated equally. The others would have to reconcile their dinners for themselves.

We hungrily devour what are, to the best of our knowledge, our menu selections and the food actually tastes pretty good. Of course, by now the culinary bar has been lowered to the point that we, along with the few remaining customers, are beginning to empathize with the survivors of the Donner Expedition.

## All Good Things...

We sit back, trying to digest our food and the dizzying events of the evening. The check arrives, surprisingly accurate and – not so surprisingly – the only thing that arrives in a timely manner. We pay the cashier, have a brief, if fruitless, conversation with Diogenes, and leave our waitress a "tip" to pursue other career options.

# WE, THE JURY

"We have a criminal jury system which is superior to any in
the world; and its efficiency is only marred by the difficulty of
finding twelve men every day
who don't know anything and can't read."
– Mark Twain

**Like other hard-working**, patriotic Americans unable to weasel out of jury duty, I've served on juries and grand juries – mostly in White Plains, New York, a pleasant 45-minute drive from my home in Yorktown Heights. However one year the Commissioner of Jurors, in his infinite wisdom, decided I could better fulfill my civic obligations in Federal Court at Foley Square, a lower Manhattan location whose distance from my Northern Westchester home is measured in light years.

## A Fun Trip

On my first day of service, I drove to the train station, parked my car, and took Metro North Railroad to Grand Central Station. (This was before the 1990s when New York City Mayor, Rudolph Guiliani, cleaned it up.) At the time of my trek, this hub of urban transit had morphed from a grand crossroads to a dimly lit underground cesspool reeking of stale, and not-so-stale, urine – and more, much more.

I stepped over bodies in every conceivable position and dodged beer bottles, wine-guzzlers, and unkempt "financial advisors." Then I took the local subway a few miles deeper into the Heart of (urban) Darkness.

After traveling for three plus hours, concluding with some clumsy plodding through wind-driven snow, I staggered into the courthouse to the area just outside the assembly room and sat in an alcove with the other chosen people, all of whom wished the Commissioner had chosen someone else. I filled out the required forms and tried to dry off.

Finally I spotted a coffee machine. *Ah! Hot coffee!* At least I could..."Out of Order." It figured.

## And the Lucky Winners Are...

We handed in our paperwork and were directed into the cavernous assembly room for roll call. Then a court official announced the names of the lucky winners who would comprise the pool for Jury Number 1. I hoped I wouldn't be chosen, but, of course, my name was called for the first case.

So I altered my hopes. Maybe I'd be subjected to a very brief trial. Perhaps I'd be assigned an interesting dispute, although it would have to be pretty damned fascinating to justify my Odyssean journey.

I obediently lined up with the other Lotto winners and together we marched forth to confront our destinies.

## Here Come the Judge!

We entered a large courtroom where we dutifully took our seats in the jury box. Then the bailiff announced: "All rise. In the case of Rufus vs. Dufus, the Honorable Judge George Clooney presiding."

*Are you kidding?*

His Honor, who looked old enough to have ruled on Marbury vs. Madison, painstakingly made his way to the bench. As he ascended the steps leading to his seat, the judge stumbled over his judicial robe. "Bailiff, I want that step fixed!"

"Yes, Your Honor."

"Be seated."

We sat. I was starting to get some really bad vibes.

Judge Clooney introduced himself, welcomed us, and gave a brief description of the case. Unfortunately, his description was the only aspect of this trial that promised to be brief. His Honor leaned forward, wagged his forefinger, and warned, "This will be a long trial. Don't make any plans in the near future."

The judge appeared to be somewhat deaf and more than a bit distracted – intent on meting out justice to a buzzing insect that hovered about him, occasionally straying onto his bench.

## The Name Game

Judge Clooney introduced the attorneys: "Mr. Kleinberg will be the prosecuting attorney."

"That's Kleinbaum, Your Honor."

"What?"

"Kleinbaum, Your Honor."

"That's Attorney Kleinbaum," the judge sternly advised us.

Buzz...

Whack!

"Mr. Chang will represent the defense," Judge Clooney continued.

"Chung, Your Honor," the attorney timidly corrected.

"What?"

"Chung."

"Yes, Mr. Chang."

"Chung."

"Chang."

"Chung."

# The Final Countdown

"I'm going to begin the selection process, Your Honor," Attorney Kleinbaum announced.

"What?"

"I'm beginning jury selection."

"Counselor, begin jury selection."

"Thank you, Your Honor."

Whack! "Yes!"

"This is where we select the jurors who will determine this case," Kleinbaum explained.

"What?"

"We will select the jurors for this case."

"Mr. Kleinman, please select the jurors."

"Uh, yes, Your Honor."

We were individually interrogated in turn by the D.A. and the defense attorney. Each began by reintroducing himself, no doubt relishing the opportunity to hear his name pronounced correctly.

All interrogations began with the same question: "Have you ever met or had any contact with me, the other attorney, His Honor, or anyone connected with this case?" This was apparently a major concern, except to Hizzoner, who was intent on entrapping, convicting, and sentencing another criminal fly.

My entire focus was on how I could get myself rejected from this ominously dark comedy and return to the real world. However, as the selection process rolled on, I abandoned all thoughts of pretending to be unqualified to serve, since they had already accepted two serial killers, a drug dealer, and a duck. There was no way to avoid the tangled web closing in on me.

# Food for Thought

After rounds of interminable questioning, most of which had to be respectfully repeated for Hizzonor, one of the attorneys suggested we break for lunch.

"What?"

"I'd like to break for lunch, Your Honor."

"What?"

The entire jury box chimed in as if on cue: "Break for lunch!"

"We should break for lunch," Hizzonor decided. "There's a lot to do this afternoon." The judge then faced the jurors, and with a stern and steady voice, forefinger in full-wag mode, warned us all, at great length, to avoid contact with the attorneys. "Dismissed!" Whack! "Got him!"

As we left the court, I clearly understood that any interaction with the attorneys was a real concern. A dim ray of hope slowly reappeared and I dared to dream I might yet avoid being sucked into the black hole of Judge Clooney's courtroom.

My subversive actions couldn't be blatant; they'd seen it all before. There would have to be no suspicion of deliberate deception or guile. This called for something subtle, something clumsy, something incredibly stupid – and I was just the one to do it.

After quickly descending two flights of stairs leading to the cafeteria, I looked at the food and realized I was starving. I also realized that one of the attorneys stood, somewhat distracted, at the end of the food line, tray in hand.

I noticed the unused trays neatly stacked in the center of the cafeteria, completely out of sight – unless you were actually looking for them or accidentally turned your eyes in their direction or were being resuscitated anywhere in the room. Just in case you had inadvertently misplaced your brain or had undergone a lobotomy and now possessed the mind of a sofa, there was also a sign the size of a wall mural: TRAYS.

Throwing self-esteem to the wind, I feigned a state of confusion and approached the familiar figure no longer at the end of the line. "Excuse me," I said to the attorney. "Where did you get the tray?"

The answer came through clenched teeth. "I can't talk to you."

"I don't want to talk to you," I said. "I just want to get a tray."

My subject, resembling an exasperated ventriloquist, repeated: "I said I can't talk."

Once I felt confident that enough people had witnessed our meaningless conversation, I shrugged my shoulders and backed off. "Thanks anyway," I said, pretending to scour the room.

"Oh, there they are!" I exclaimed, seeming to finally notice the elephant in the room. I approached the stack of unused trays, grabbed one, and walked to the end of the ever-growing line. After purchasing a sandwich and a bottle of water, I sat at one of the now crowded tables. Paul Winchell had long since made a hasty retreat from the cafeteria.

## To Please the Court

When we reconvened in the courtroom, Judge Clooney asked the attorneys to continue the selection process. Immediately, my reluctant cafeteria confidant stood and requested a peremptory challenge. "If it pleases Your Honor..."

"What?"

Raising his voice: "If it pleases the court, I would like to dismiss Juror Number Nine."

A hidden fist pump. *"Yes!"*

"Juror Number Nine, you are dismissed! Return to the assembly room," Judge Clooney announced. Obsessed with leaving before anyone could question my unexpected good fortune, I tripped over several jurors-in-waiting as I initiated my hasty retreat.

When I reached the door, I listened to the sounds of our criminal justice system in action:

"Blah! Blah! Blah!"

"What?" "What?" "What?"

Whack!

At four-thirty we were dismissed from the assembly room and sent home. I assumed my former fellow detainees in the courtroom were still fidgeting in their seats and stealing glances at their watches. But I headed home to end what would be a 14-hour day, one in which I had accomplished - nothing. Mercifully, I was not called to "serve" again in Judge Clooney's theater of the absurd.

## Staying Civil

I've since learned that my county allows for volunteer jury service, enabling me to perform my civic duty at a courthouse within four zip codes of my home, which is what I have done in the years following my lower Manhattan experience. Meanwhile, downtown in the bowels of the city, I knew at least one magistrate was waging his peculiar war on crime with unwarranted conviction. I'm sure Hizzoner faithfully continued doling out justice to deviants, malcontents, and psychopaths, as well as to vagrant insects who brazenly dared to invade his courtroom.

# FAMILY VACATIONS:
# A TALE OF TWO BROTHERS

"It is not worthwhile to go around the world to count the cats in Zanzibar."
– Henry David Thoreau

**My brother and I are lifelong best friends** who share the same moral, political, and social values. However, we will never be caught sharing mutual vacation time. But more about my brother later.

## It's a Vacation, Dammit!

To me, a vacation is an opportunity to get away. It's about our plane reaching the designated landing field and having that be one of the last things designated for the next seven or eight days. It's about going to a place that offers unstructured peace and comfort and asks for nothing in return. In my land of discarded timepieces, there's no pressing need to plan my next move or even know what I'm going to do – or not going to do – or where or when I'm not going to do it.

The more "You gotta see this!" sites and "Don't miss this!" landmarks I can avoid, the better. I have no desire to visit the Raging Rapids of Ronconcomo, the Sagging Sycamores of Singapore, or the home of the first gastroenterologist to isolate the fart.

However, there is a fuzzy routine to my typical vacation

day. It begins – not too early – with a long, leisurely breakfast, overlooking absolutely nothing but more breakfast. Then I'm off to find a comfortable chair in the shade where I can read, write, sleep, listen to music or shamelessly gawk at the scantily clad sun-worshippers gathered around the pool or stretched out on the beach.

My wife of forty-plus years, who still turns my eye and continues to wear her bathing suit quite well, is – for the most part – unthreatened by my cerebral escapades. ("As long as you keep them cerebral!") She understands that I, like a former president, lust only in my mind – unlike another former Commander-in-Chief who, in the Oval Office, stretched the pleasures of diplomatic immunity (among other things) to its limits.

While I'm relaxing in the shade and, perhaps, entertaining some shady thoughts, my better half is happily lapping up the sun and enjoying the pristine waters of the ocean, lake, or pool. We're usually within waving distance and, if not, she will break routine and walk over to say "hello" and mention, incidentally, that she has left her bathing cap, suntan lotion, or crossword puzzle in the room. This not-so-subtle hint invariably happens at the climax of a chapter or at the very moment an intent sun-worshipper decides to even out her tan.

## Stick to the Tropic

I remember our first trip to Aruba – the land of cooling trade winds, endless white-sand beaches, tantalizing restaurants, and delightfully few places of interest. While my wife is hungrily soaking up the Caribbean sun, I'm reading/sleeping under one of four shade trees living out its lonely existence in two miles of barren Aruban sand.

As I'm nodding (nearly napping), a vision of feminine perfection – as if from the uncensored regions of my mind –

appears. She places a folding chair under the not-so-far-side of my tree and casually removes the upper half of her barely visible swimsuit. (I'm unaware if this is acceptable behavior under Aruban law, but reporting her to the authorities is not an option.)

Now I'm wide-awake. She unfolds her chair and her magazine, lies down, and begins soaking up the shade. I adjust my shades to look like I'm actually reading the book I hold upside down on my lap.

## I've missed you too

My wife, who has apparently decided we've been separated too long, abruptly appears at my side, turns my book right side up, surveys my questionable surroundings, and, keeping her voice under control, demands: "Is this the only place on the beach you could find to put your chair?"

After I gather my senses and explain that I was here first, she has the audacity to suggest that I should have – moved!

"You're kidding!" I stammer in wide-eyed disbelief. "There isn't another shade tree in this zip code." Besides, a voluntary retreat would be an insult to my gender. How do I explain? It's a guy thing. We're not bred to seek refuge when confronted by a breathtaking vision and we certainly don't look for a less distracting place to read.

My mildly offended spouse steals one last disapproving glance at my voluptuous neighbor and, with a dismissive wave of her hand, returns to her sandy altar to resume worshiping the Aruban sun gods while I resume my unrepentant gawking at my goddess of the shade.

## Just look at those...

My reverie is abruptly interrupted when my personal Hooters Playmate of the Decade – the enchanting object of

157

what's-her-name's objections – inexplicably jumps up and yells, "Look! Look!"

My jaw and my book drop simultaneously as I wonder how to assure her I've been looking as hard as I could.

She points to the sky as she repeats the most unnecessary command since, "Run Forrest, run!"

Somehow I manage to unhinge my eyes long enough to notice two huge, ominously dark clouds drifting toward us.

She snaps on her bikini top with incredible swiftness – considering the daunting nature of the task – folds her chair and heads for the roofed refuge of a nearby concession stand. I leap out of my chair, trip on my book, fall on my ass, and gracelessly stumble to the same place of shelter. There, I reunite with my wife, who, thankfully, appears more concerned with solar deprivation than spousal rumination. Later I tell her the rest of the story, which we will forever refer to as my "'Look! Look!' Experience."

## It's a Vacation! (continued)

But I digress. My typical vacation day: reading, writing, eating, sleeping – the sun and the shade, the waving and the visiting, perhaps a (short) walk on the beach. In the evening we eat a leisurely dinner, check out the local entertainment, try our luck in the casino, refresh ourselves with some island concoctions, purchase a few souvenirs (of places we didn't visit) – whatever strikes our fancy. It's a vacation!

## Oh, Brother! An Opposing View

And then there's my brother Harvey (name changed to protect Howard's identity). For "Harvey," the planning stage of a vacation requires the precision of a well-coordinated, multi-lateral military operation. He locks himself in his self-imposed

"War Room" and ponders: How much time do I have? What is there for me to see and explore? How many activities can I fit into my time frame? Which activities can I squeeze between these activities without experiencing temporary blackouts or passing out completely?

Fortunately, his wife, June (not Jane), shares Harvey's penchant for recreational exhaustion. Together they have crammed weeks of sightseeing madness into mere days of scheduled vacation time. Planned activities inevitably evolve into an unspoken competition to determine who can maintain consciousness the longest before falling into his or her food.

## And Away We Go!

A few years ago, Harvey and June embarked on a whirlwind one-week Hawaiian vacation, which, sadly, had to be pared down from the scheduled two-week adventure meticulously micro-planned in the War Room. However, not wanting to eliminate an island or any of his painstakingly orchestrated activities, Harvey decided they could squeeze their agenda into the new time frame, much like squishing those last three shirts and pair of pants into an already over-packed suitcase. They would simply awaken a bit earlier, move a bit faster, and eliminate, or at least drastically reduce, any non-essential activity – like sleep.

### Stand back – It's dormant!

Early in their idyllic – if compressed – "vacation," Harvey and June woke up at three a.m. to drive to the top of a dormant volcano in Maui. There they were joined by more than a hundred other lunatics who had gathered at this ungodly hour – to see a sunrise!

As Harvey recalls, several of these sightseeing fanatics tiptoed gingerly along the site afraid that kicking a few pebbles would awaken the sleeping giant, which had for centuries withstood the ravages of time, nature, and clumsy tourists. He remembers two teenage drama queens whose every step was accompanied by a frantic, "Oh, my God!" fearing each move could unleash a flow of lava and, OMG, disrupt their hair!

I'm not questioning the intelligence of a horde of fervent vacationers who awoke at three a.m. to view a damn sunrise. But I've never felt the need to be privy to a natural occurrence that has played out daily without my attendance – especially one that happens at such an outrageous time of day. (I'm sure if I lived on a farm, I'd start each morning by strangling a rooster.)

However, Harvey and June enjoyed the experience so much they arrived for a repeat performance the following day before dawn, only to discover it was raining at the top of the mountain. With no sunrise to witness, a hundred dejected sightseers drove down the mountainside and went back to bed – all but two.

## Whale of a time

After the aborted sunrise experience, Harvey decided to make productive use of this newfound vacation time. He drove to a nearby beach – some twenty miles away (Harvey and I have never agreed on the meaning of "nearby"), which they had been told was an ideal location for – whale watching!

To Harvey's and June's amazement, the beach was quite empty – a testament to the relative sanity of the other sightseers, who had passed on the opportunity to sit on a desolate beach at four a.m. to witness virtually indiscernible dots on the horizon, which they would later claim to have been whales.

## Grin and Bear It

As if wearing himself (and his faithful, if misguided, wife) to a frazzle didn't provide sufficient satisfaction, Harvey decided a true vacation must include an element of danger. He concluded that putting himself in harm's way would keep him feeling young or at least help him grow old gracefully, never entertaining the possibility that he might be compromising his opportunity to actually experience old age.

So the year after their Hawaiian "vacation," the adventuresome duo took off for Alaska. Harvey found a remote location called Broken Falls, where they would be trained in the protocol for encountering the wild grizzlies that shared their vacation resort. In Bear School, students were taught to chatter loudly when entering suspected bear territory to alert the bears that humans were approaching. This made perfect sense, especially to the man-eating grizzlies – kind of like the "Come and get it!" dinner chimes of the Old West.

However, Harvey and his fellow adventurers were assured the river provided abundant food and the bears posed no danger, unless they felt threatened. If students encountered a bear, they were instructed to walk backwards, talk calmly to the bear ("Hello, bear..."), avoid getting between a mother and her cub and, above all, never to panic.

After learning the basic protocols, the group was deemed ready to explore the region. Unfortunately for this Bear School graduating class, their novice tour guide was lacking in basic grizzly etiquette and, at the first bear sighting, yelled, "Bear!" and ran for the safety of the gated viewing platform on the bridge, leaving his petrified troops to fend for themselves.

Fortunately, the bear, apparently sated on salmon, continued its stroll and showed little interest in the not-ready-for-prime-time troop leader or his followers, to the relief of

Harvey and the other forsaken fun-seekers who proceeded towards the bridge to join the inadvertent new world record holder for the 40-yard dash.

As the group intently observed the bears in the river catching and eating salmon, my brother and several others who had disdained the suggested protective netting, observed themselves being eaten by giant mosquitoes and black flies. These flying creatures, my brother astutely noticed, weren't common New York nippy mosquitoes. Instead, they were three-inch-long predators that left nasty welts on virtually all exposed skin. (Alaskans refer to the mosquito as their unofficial state bird.) But I'm sure the experience of being eaten alive only added to the thrill of their questionable commune with nature.

## Looking Ahead

Now Harvey and June are talking about taking an African safari, where the insects make Alaskan mosquitoes look like aphids. When I learned of this latest enterprise, I decided to spare the aspiring adventurers the inconvenience of attending "Lion School." Instead, I researched the protocol for interaction with the "kings of beasts" they might encounter on their jungle jaunt:

* If you confront a lion during mating season, you must immediately relinquish your mate.

This is considered a gesture of good will and most lions will allow the relinquisher to live. The relinquishee, however, is in for a long night.

* Begin eating anything resembling vegetation as quickly as possible.

By doing this, you will not be perceived as a competitor for the carnivore's food supply. Unfortunately, this will not eliminate the possibility of you being perceived as food.

* If possible, dive into a body of water.

Lions are reluctant swimmers. However, you must then immediately initiate the protocol for facing a crocodile.
* If you see two lions fighting, do not stop to photograph them.
They are probably fighting over who gets to eat you.
* Finally, if you feel the need to relieve yourself, remember this is how lions mark their territory.
Therefore, they might consider your actions offensive. (Unfortunately, when facing a lion in the wild, relieving oneself is often an involuntary action.)

*

I hope Harvey heeds my well-intentioned suggestions when he and June embark on their next intricately-planned vacation. As for me, I'm still looking for that perfectly shaded stretch of sand under a tree on some secluded beach without a dress code.

# TO MY HEALTH

# A SHOT IN THE ASS

"This was the most unkindest cut of all."
– William Shakespeare

**There is a pithy truism** that should be inscribed among the axioms of the ages: "Jews shall not build their own flagstone patios." I learned this the hard way as a much younger man and, over the years, my offended Hebrew back has been a daily reminder of my ethnic-defying hubris.

After consulting an endless array of orthopedists, acupuncturists, chiropractors, orthodontists, cosmetologists, endocrinologists, proctologists, and a few well-intentioned snake oil merchants, I settled on my current – and hopefully last – spine-bender, a highly recommended local chiropractor, with an upscale office in Manhattan. Following two excruciatingly painful sessions where he was unable to unhinge my inflexible back, he ordered an epidural injection at a major New York City hospital to loosen the lumbar.

## The Let-Me-Out Patients

I checked into the hospital as an outpatient, completed the required forms, and impatiently waited in a waiting room full of kvetchers, whiners, and grumblers who, without provocation, enthusiastically shared their hard-luck stories.

Seeing me "ease" into a vacant chair, my face contorted in pain, one perceptive sleuth inquired, "Bad back, huh?"

"No," I replied. "Selecting a proper chair has always been an emotional experience for me."

Finally, I was led into a large room of many beds, curtained off, but unfortunately not sound-proof. Didn't anyone keep their problems to themselves anymore?

"That's a big needle."

"You ain't sticking me with that!"

"Your hands are cold."

"Is this gonna hurt?"

## The Numb and the Restless

As "just a few minutes" turned into the next calendar month, I received the appropriate doses of Novacaine, Dalmane, Butane, Lipotain, Solarcaine, and Rogaine, and got myself epiduralized.

My first question after the procedure, phrased as diplomatically as possible was, "When can I get the ____ out of here?"

A matronly, post-menopausal, and remarkably well-nourished nurse (the guy in the next bed got the pretty, young one) told me to relax until I felt well enough to get up. Then she adjusted my feet, fluffed my pillow, and patted my rump, all of which greatly enhanced my desire to bid farewell to this aggravatingly attentive mountain of comfort.

I tried relaxing until, feeling increasingly antsy, I decided it was time to hit the floor. Unfortunately, that's exactly what I did because, when I tried to stand, I had no sense of my feet touching the ground. Summoning all my strength, I attempted to mount a manly ascent to the bed, but got no further than a ridiculous semi-kneeling, helplessly groping position.

Realizing I had reached the limit of independent vertical

motion, I pushed the little red button for a nurse. When the water in my glass started to ripple and the lighting in the room grew dim, I knew I would once again be at the mercy of the Queen of Triglicerides.

When she finally arrived, with the urgency of an inebriated sloth, Nurse Malomar hoisted me into bed and explained that numbness in the legs was a normal reaction to the epidural procedure. She told me to wait until the feeling in my lower extremities returned, patted my rump yet again *(Some sort of fetish?)* and left a sheet of paper on the nightstand.

"Read this when you get a chance," she said as she exited, thus gradually allowing adequate reading light to again filter into the room.

Since I wasn't busy, I picked up the paper, which contained a list of post-epidural expectations and caveats – thought-provoking professional insights, obviously gathered after years of medical research and astute observation: "Following the epidural, you may experience numbness in the legs and a dull pain in the ass."

*Yes, I've met her.*

"Do not attempt to walk, bend over, sprint, lift heavy objects, engage in sexual activity *(with who?)*, try out for the Green Bay Packers..."

Not that I needed an additional incentive to bid my fond adieus, but the serial kvetchers were awakening. Apparently the novacaine and sedatives were wearing off and the malcontents were getting louder and more persistent. The voices seemed to be increasing. Were there more of them? Were they breeding?

"Where the hell am I?"

"Who are you?"

"I can't reach my water glass."

"Is this gonna hurt?"

## Don't Stop Me Now!

I desperately needed to put some distance between myself and this medically-approved cuckoo's nest. I had to move my ass – or at least my legs. Sasquatch had said to wait until the senses there returned, but since it was difficult to evaluate the degree of numbness while lying in bed and I wasn't quite ready for another Fosbury Flop, I resorted to banging my legs against the bedposts to evoke some sort of sensation.

After many fruitless revival attempts, I finally felt a somewhat fruitful tingling and positioned myself for takeoff and the possibility of another inglorious landing. However, this time I was able to unravel into a standing position without help from the human forklift. I struggled into my clothes and, with list in hand, wished everyone a good afternoon, trying my best to give the impression of a man capable of exiting under his own power.

## To Piss or Not to...

My first stop was a long anticipated trip to the men's room. (I refused to have Clara Barton-Barricini assist me with my bodily functions.) But to my dismay, not only was I unable to pee, I couldn't even feel the unresponsive organ lying shamelessly comatose in my hand.

I looked at my list and found no mention of this latest dilemma. Do not "engage in sexual activity." *Thanks for the head's up*. Perusing the sheet was no mean task since I needed to hold onto the wall, the list, and my disappointing appendage – in case it suddenly returned to life.

After a few frantic moments of stroking, cajoling, shaking, even slapping this delinquent slackard's head against the wall like a defiant criminal, I sadly pocketed my unrepentent prisoner and rehearsed how I would present this new unnerving episode to an attending nurse. Youth and beauty were no longer relevant; for this I wanted a nurse who looked like a nurse.

## Um...Here's the Problem

I swallowed my devastated ego, and, on wobbly legs, abandoned the restroom and reluctantly returned to the scene of the crime. I approached a nurse who had obviously been around the block, if not the entire borough, and who seemed to be out of earshot of other personnel. When I clumsily explained that I couldn't even feel it when I tried to urinate, she assured me this was not uncommon and "it" would soon go away altogether. Now I was suffering from a problem with semantics.

As the look on my face revealed my latest concern, she reassured me all systems would return to normal within the hour. I suggested that my experience should be added to the post-epidural awareness sheet to head off the likelihood of major panic attacks or acts of desperation by future victims of the procedure.

## A Rude Awakening

I left the hospital and, as I drove along the Taconic Parkway, somewhere between Pleasantville and Ossining the tiger in my tank began to purr. However, the joy of once again bonding with my old companion was short-lived as the urge to relieve myself returned with a vengeance.

Many of our nation's highways take into consideration the need for an emergency stopover. Unfortunately, the Taconic isn't one of them. Realizing I would never make it home, or even to the next exit, I pulled over, knelt down, and with my back to traffic, took the matter into my own hands – in a manner of speaking. Then I returned to my car ready to complete the drive home. But I was no longer alone.

"Yes, Officer? Well, it all started with a patio."

# NO PLACE LIKE OM

"Blessed are the flexible for they shall not be bent
out of shape."
– Anonymous

**For years, my daughter raved** about the therapeutic wonders of yoga. It would make me more flexible and help me to relax and unwind, she insisted in an ongoing attempt to extricate me from the ranks of the omless.

I finally caved in and joined a class at a local yoga center. Of course, I was entering the arena not as an energetic 30-something, but as an arthritic, lower-lumbar compromised, medically-challenged sexagenarian.

My daughter, however, was excited for me. "When I started, I could hardly touch the floor," she said. "Now I can bend over straight-kneed and easily pick a penny off the ground. You'll be able to do that too, Dad."

"Not for a hundred dollar bill, sweetheart."

But what was there to lose? I envisioned yoga as a relaxing, meditative experience practiced by Buddhist monks and other sedentary creatures. And I could use some relaxing techniques and therapeutic flexibility in my life.

## A "Gentle" Beginning

At the owner/instructor's suggestion, I embarked on my

journey towards eternal health and tranquility by joining the "Gentle Yoga" class. She assured me this class would "increase flexibility, improve breathing habits, enhance relaxation, and improve sleep." Why had I waited so long?

As my first class was about to begin, we sat Indian-style on our mats in front of the group leader. "Your hips should be above your knees," she announced softly. "If necessary, sit on a blanket to increase comfort and to raise your hips."

Since my crossed legs placed my knees near ear level, I had to sit on so many blankets I found myself in a near-standing position. But the dull pain in my back seemed to be relenting and I approached some degree of comfort – though I was situated conspicuously higher than my classmates.

"Relax all your muscles," the leader continued. "Focus on your breathing. Listen to your breath. Forget your problems. Don't think about your drive here."

*I got lost.*

"Don't fret about money problems."

*I just got a bill for…*

"Don't worry about the bad weather we're experiencing."

*My pipes are frozen.*

"Stay in the moment. Don't think about what you're going to do when you leave."

*I'm calling a plumber.*

Somehow, I wasn't very relaxed. My breathing came in short, tight spurts. I was pissed. *What's the first damn move?*

"Now get on your hands and knees."

*I can do that.*

"Assume the Downward Dog position."

This move involved raising your ass as high as possible with hands and feet touching the floor.

"Lift your right leg and swing it forward until your right foot rests alongside your right hand."

This was not a smooth maneuver for me since I had to use my left hand to drag my right foot into place. But I did it. *Now how am I going to extricate myself from this position, which is already beyond anything...*

"Push your left arm under your chin until it touches your right shoulder."

I looked around and saw two women who had actually mastered this move. The guy next to me repeatedly stabbed at his right shoulder with his left hand before finally falling on his face.

I was stuck. Apparently, I was going to topple over and land on my back like a bug. After completing my version of this Kafkaesque pose, I tried to pick up the instructor's words, hoping we were going to explore a more restful position. But no such luck.

## Not "Dogging" It

The lesson continued with hardly a pause: "Now repeat with your left leg."

A disturbing request, since that was my only remaining appendage with circulation.

"Begin by returning to Downward Dog. Remember to use Downward Dog as a restful, relaxing, position whenever necessary. Now swing your left leg..."

For me, Downward Dog was as relaxing as holding on to the hood of a getaway car. I would learn that Downward Dog was but one of a host of animal-inspired yoga positions. (Why wasn't I suspicious of a discipline with poses named for eagles, cows, monkeys, turtles, seals, pigeons, lions, camels, fish, cobras, peacocks, cranes, and scorpions?)

I would also learn that for Downward Dog, medical clearance is suggested for those with injury to the back, arms, or shoulders or anyone with high blood pressure, heart issues, or glaucoma. This caveat sounded eerily like my medical history.

## Let's Do the Twist

"Place your right leg behind your neck so the sole of your foot is facing the wall to your left. Place your left leg under your left arm and lean back..."

I noticed that no matter how bizarre the position, the instructor's voice never strayed from the same calm, inflectionless tone.

"Stick your left hand up your ass until you feel a gentle pressure against the inside of your right eye. Push your left foot down your throat until it touches your left elbow. If any of this feels at all uncomfortable, don't force it."

*Everything after swallowing my foot...*

"Slide your right hand past your trachea, along the duodenum, until you can touch your pancreas. Grab your pancreas and slowly draw it towards your spleen. Continue breathing normally."

*My spleen?*

*What could she possibly do to end the insanity? Surely the grand finale will involve setting the class on fire.*

## Peace at Last

The instructor mercifully ended the session with the fittingly named "Corpse Pose," the one position I could still execute. "Lay on your backs, hands at your sides, and close your eyes," she whispered. "We are about to experience a period of quiet meditation. Close your eyes," she repeated, "and concentrate only on your breathing."

Relieved to be still capable of aspiration, labored though it might be, I assumed the assigned pose, and effortlessly portrayed the barely animate corpse into which I had evolved.

*Where the hell is my spleen?*

"Imagine your material possessions fluttering away," the Corpse Whisperer continued. "All you are left with is the tranquil sound of your breathing. Just focus on the soothing rhythm of your breath. Shut out all sounds of the outside world. Disregard the rustling noises in the back of the room where you left your outer garments. Dismiss all thoughts of material possessions and concentrate on your inner self."

I later learned that while I was focusing on my inner self, a yogi in the rear was methodically relieving me of my wallet, phone, and other material possessions.

## A Fond Adieu

I'm sure yoga has its virtues and holds a special place in the lives of its many devotees, but perhaps some of us weren't meant to assume exotic poses to help us relax, meditate, and breathe our troubles away. So I bade my final farewell to "Downward Dog," "Catatonic Cow," "Reclining Turtle," "Herniated Wolf," "Demented Pig," "Meshugginah Mouse," and the other players in this perverted Animal Farm and resigned myself to seeking more conventional ways of coping with the complexities of my life.

# WITH A SIDE OF EFFECTS – TO GO

"The cure is worse than the disease."
– Philip Massinger

**Long ago, when a doctor** prescribed a new medication, I asked, with the youthful innocence of a 39-year-old: "Will there be any side effects?"

His answer: "You get nothing for nothing."

So simple, yet so true. You relieve this; you get that. Medically speaking, we live in a "nothing for nothing" world. Every remedy comes with its own hidden price tag. The piper must be paid!

## Be Not Still My Heart

Over the years, I've often been reminded of the good doctor's parting words, most recently after a coronary angiogram. As the nurse filled out the Discharge Instruction Sheet, I asked her about potential side effects.

Without looking up, she matter-of-factly explained that if I noticed bleeding from the incision (in the groin area, no less) I should apply pressure and, if the bleeding continued, call 911, since, in three minutes, I could possibly bleed to death.

*Hey, lady! Are we being a bit too casual here?* An image flashed through my mind: Holding a bloody towel, I frantically call 911, am put on hold, and hear this message: "Waiting time will be approximately three minutes."

"OK," I said, emerging from my disturbing fantasy. "Anything else I should know?"

"Well, I don't have your medical history," she calmly resumed, "but a coronary angiogram is somewhat invasive, so there's always the chance of a heart attack."

Wait a minute! Let me get this straight. The possible "side effects" of this relatively routine procedure are death by bleeding and a potentially fatal heart attack. I had hoped to hear something like, "You might experience a runny nose and a slight tingling sensation."

Upon further questioning, Nurse Ratchet dismissed these ghastly reactions as highly unlikely worst-case scenarios and proceeded to write the more common side effects on the discharge sheet – mostly something about redness and soreness at the point of entry. Somehow, these last two far more likely by-products of the procedure were immediately forgotten as I was wheeled from the recovery room.

During the weeks that followed, I was neither bloodied nor stricken. There wasn't even much redness or soreness. I did, however, have a bit of a runny nose.

## Side Effects May Include...

These days we are programmed to be more aware of side effects than ever before – a logical consequence of the rampant TV ads for an endless array of medical remedies. (This is probably because we Baby Boomers, always a major demographic, are now up there in age and are seen as more receptive to pills than thrills.)

Ads for the holy grail of instant relief suggest that by taking some medical elixir, you will relive the gaiety of walking through an island of flowers, the joy of playing with your children and grandchildren, and the exhilaration of once again jogging along your favorite wooded trail. But this temporary euphoria is immediately followed by a litany of mandatory disclaimers.

I become uneasy when the warnings last far longer than the descriptions and testimonials. In fact, the seemingly interminable caveats often dwarf the product information. Many even appear to rival the worst possible scenarios of my post-angiogram scare.

These unnerving disclaimers start off slowly and gradually build to their disturbing climax: "With Antisuffrin you may experience a temporary upset stomach or a raspy throat."

*Fine. I'll try it. Now let's see what's on Channel...But wait; there's more.*

"Some people have reported abdominal pain, blurry vision, or poor bowel control."

*Hey, maybe it's not worth...*

"Notify your doctor immediately if you experience loss of equilibrium, general confusion, or an inability to identify family members or your own body parts."

*Those are not side effects; those are some butt-ugly effects!*

"In rare cases, people have been known to explode."

By now, I've completely forgotten why I was interested in this particular medication, but whatever condition it was intended to cure I've decided to live with.

Some tradeoffs, while less dramatic, fail to withstand even the most casual scrutiny. If I'm taking a pill for stomach distress, why should one possible side effect be an upset stomach? Is the upset stomach I may get from your pill better than the upset stomach I had in the first place? This could be the same upset stomach I had before, but now it's a side effect of a pill for an upset stomach.

What about the person with bladder control problems?

"Take P-No-More and you will regain control of your bladder – but you could experience severe stomach cramps and violent diarrhea."

So now instead of needing to take an urgent piss in a crowded movie theater or on a slow-moving bus, you may succumb to an immediate and uncontrollable need to shit your pants.

## Caveats for a New Era

In our rapidly shrinking world, a new breed of admonitions has recently emerged. "Before taking Hypobarfaside, tell your doctor if you have ever had the Ketchmir Virus, or have traveled to a country which has been infected by this virus, or have come in contact with someone who's been to a country with Ketchmir, or have read about a country where Ketchmir is prevalent, or have visited a country that does business with an infected country, or have visited your mother. If not, she probably wants to hear from you, unless you have recently returned from or have ever visited a foreign country..."

## The Hard Life

Remember the Marlboro Man? Back in the '50s and '60s, when the tough guys smoked cigarettes after a manly cattle drive, this epitome of the rugged outdoorsman would bring his horse to a screeching halt and light up – like a real man.

In today's world, the horrific health tolls of cigarette smoking are common knowledge so we (hopefully) no longer idolize smokers. As a result, the virile, tobacco-sucking Marlboro Man has lost much of his charisma.

Not to worry – Marlboro Man has been replaced by E.D. Man. This modern day rugged outdoorsman climbs mountainous terrain, repairs tractors and boats with minimal tools, throws a football through a spare tire with the accuracy of Joe Montana, and cleans up a barroom brawl with the virility of John Wayne. Unfortunately, E.D. Man, for all his manly virtues, has one enduring problem: He can't get it up.

But now there's Stiff 'n' Hard. You take Stiff 'n' Hard as needed or once daily so you can be a manly man whenever the time is right – in the sack, on a boat, on the tractor, or after a cattle drive.

For all we know, Marlboro Man may have been an earlier version of E.D. Man. But with Stiff 'n' Hard, his wife could have hung her laundry on it. He could have tied his horse to it. I'm sure Marlboro Man would have disdained the traditional hitching post and fastened his steed to his personal ramrod had he known about Stiff 'n' Hard.

Ah, but remember the good doctor's warning: "You get nothing for nothing." So here come the disclaimers:

"In addition to headache, upset stomach, low blood pressure, and general disorientation, you may experience prolonged blurry vision and drastically diminished hearing." Plus, there is a chance that after a few minutes of experimenting with Stiff 'n' Hard, you could lose your horse.

\*

Do not go out and party too soon after taking Stiff 'n' Hard to show off your attractive new bulge or you might participate in this conversation:

Pretty Young Thing: "Oh my, you must take Stiff 'n' Hard!"
You: "What did you say? Where are you?"

\*

"If you get an erection that lasts for more than four hours, call your doctor immediately!"

For what?

*

Of course, remember: "Don't take Stiff 'n' Hard if you are taking nitrates."

Right! What the hell are nitrates?

*

There's one final warning from E.D. Man or his smugly satisfied partner: "Before taking Stiff 'n' Hard, check with your doctor to see if your heart is strong enough for sexual activity."

This drug could last for hours and it's not like you know how you're going to "hold up" (medically) after awakening the dead. We're talking about someone who hasn't gotten any for weeks, months, maybe years. But when opportunity arises (along with...), most of these newly empowered riverboat gamblers will, like true cowboys, chance an early exit in the saddle – and "let it ride."

## FYI

Sometimes potential side effects are listed on the label and are about as illuminating as "Don't mix with rat poison." Sleeping pills come with this written caveat: "May cause drowsiness."

They're supposed to cause drowsiness. They're sleeping pills! If I take a sleeping pill, I want to fall into a six to eight hour coma-like sleep.

"Do not drive or operate heavy machinery after taking Super Snooze."

It's a sleeping pill! Anyone who takes a damn sleeping pill before approaching the Interstate or operating a forklift is severely weakening the gene pool.

*

For medications that dry you out, the label reads: "While taking this medication, drink plenty of fluids." I can only suppose this is intended for those of us who drink sand.

## Time for Your Meds

Once you've nailed down the pros and cons of your wonder drugs, don't expect to chow them down at your convenience. You are instructed to take your medication –

* first thing in the morning
* just before going to sleep at night
* with food
* on an empty stomach
* thirty minutes after your last meal
* one hour before your first meal
* twelve hours after citrus fruit
* with stringy vegetables
* two – three hours before anticipated onset of pain (How the hell do I know...?)

Set the timer, honey.

## Careful, Careful...

Finally, in a blatant attempt to cover their corporate asses, additional words of caution warn against accidental mishaps: "When taking Lung-Gevity, don't stand up too quickly. Don't sit down at all. Don't brush your teeth. Don't talk to strangers..."

Obviously, these meds should only be administered in a health care facility, where a professionally trained staff can monitor you before and after you have taken the latest wonder drug.

*

Perhaps Mel Brooks, as the lovable Two Thousand-Year-Old Man, had the answer. Long ago, if you were sick or got hurt, you'd just lie down and stay there until you either got better or died.

# AFTERWARD

So what have I learned from my "novel" experience, other than I'm not a novelist? I learned to hold on to my dreams, even if I must modify them along the way. I never became a novelist, but I married one. And I finally wrote the book I was meant to write.

To dare to dream, to enjoy a good laugh – these are the traits that separate us from frogs and toads – these plus a warty skin and the ability to catch flies.

I hope you enjoyed the book. If so, I'd enjoy hearing from you at my wife's website: www.susanberliner.com (I don't do websites.) I'd also appreciate a brief review on Amazon.

If you didn't like the book – "Ayyy!"

# APPENDIX

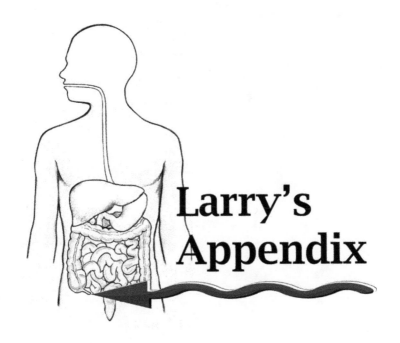

Larry's Appendix

CPSIA information can be obtained
at www.ICGtesting.com
Printed in the USA
FFHW012207310319
51354839-56842FF